PRETTY MESS

PRETTY MESS

ERIKA JAYNE

G

GALLERY BOOKS

New York   London   Toronto   Sydney   New Delhi

G

Gallery Books
An Imprint of Simon & Schuster, Inc.
1230 Avenue of the Americas
New York, NY 10020

First Gallery Books trade paperback edition February 2019

GALLERY BOOKS and colophon are registered trademarks of Simon & Schuster, Inc.

For information about special discounts for bulk purchases, please contact Simon & Schuster Special Sales at 1-866-506-1949 or business@simonandschuster.com.

The Simon & Schuster Speakers Bureau can bring authors to your live event. For more information or to book an event, contact the Simon & Schuster Speakers Bureau at 1-866-248-3049 or visit our website at www.simonspeakers.com.

Interior design by Jaime Putorti

Manufactured in the United States of America

10   9   8   7   6   5   4   3   2

Library of Congress Cataloging-in-Publication Data is available for the hardcover edition.

ISBN 978-1-5011-8189-4
ISBN 978-1-5011-8190-0 (pbk)
ISBN 978-1-5011-8191-7 (ebook)

To Ann. Wish you were here.

CONTENTS

CONTENTS

PRETTY MESS

1

EVE HARRINGTON FROM THE START

I made my stage debut at the age of five. I was in the St. John the Baptist Kindergarten production of *Mrs. Jingle B*. It was a Christmas pageant with singing that sounded more like screaming in unison. The dancing looked like a bunch of drunk bunny rabbits trying to find their way home after a bender.

I don't exactly remember the plot of the show. I was cast as an elf, essentially relegating me to the chorus. After the first few days of rehearsal, I realized that the girl who was cast in the lead—as Mrs. Jingle B herself—was not doing a very good job.

I was very confident. I walked up to my teacher and said, "I can do a better job than her." The teacher agreed. In front of the entire kindergarten class and all of their parents, I took my star turn wearing a quilted plaid jumper, a white blouse with a Peter Pan collar, and black mary janes. I might have had my hair cut short like a boy's, but I was an Eve Harrington right from the start.

My mother, Renee, taught piano out of our house to make extra money. She is an excellent musician, but I never wanted to be one of her students. When we sat at the piano, she didn't have nearly as much patience with me as she did with her other students. I used to swat her away so I could practice on my own. This would always lead to fights between us. Eventually, when I was still very young, I lost interest in piano altogether. It was one of my ways of rebelling. Instead of learning her instrument of choice, I would let her accompany me while I sang songs and did little dance routines for our friends and family. I would become dizzy on the applause, bowing vigorously for the small crowd.

From the time I was three, before performing I would shut myself in the closet at my grandmother's house. I wouldn't come out until I'd been properly introduced. Then I'd walk into the room, hop up on the coffee table, and sing songs for the family. Mostly I did rhymes or things I had heard on my favorite TV shows, like *Mister Rogers' Neighborhood*, *Sesame Street*, or *Romper Room*. I would not allow Renee to accompany me on the piano. These were a capella productions.

I don't know where I was getting this from, but I always wanted to be a showgirl. I imagined costumes, big stages, colored lights, an announcer calling my name, and walking out there and putting on a show for the people. I wanted the full production, like an MGM musical with a moving staircase. Some people are dying to sing and some people want to dance, but my goal was always to put on a *show*.

One day when I was about three, my mother and I went to go visit her friend Anne. She lived in downtown Atlanta and would sometimes babysit me. Anne's neighbor, a woman who owned the Cheryl Neal and Associates talent agency, saw me playing by myself in the front yard.

"Is this your little girl?" she asked Renee. (I always call my mother Renee because I often saw her more as a peer.)

"Yes."

"She is just really cute and entertaining as hell," she said. "I own a talent agency. I want you to bring her in and we can see what we can do for her."

She gave my mother her card. Shortly thereafter, we went to her office and signed with her as my agent. She would send me out to castings for local commercials or TV shows that needed a cute, blond little girl. This was not the Atlanta of today, where there are hundreds of shows being produced. Everything I was going out for was very small potatoes.

Renee or my grandmother would drive me around to the auditions. As a small child, I always had a fun time, even if I didn't get the gig. I booked some of the jobs, but of course I didn't get most of them. I remember doing some local commercials and a bit of modeling.

Later, in high school, I filmed a public service announcement in which I played a girl sitting on her bed listening to her boom box. "I would love to be a rock star. I'd be famous," I said. "But some of them use drugs. And that scares me!" This was my brain on cheesy PSAs; any questions?

When I worked, my mother would get the check, and she and my grandmother would put it into a savings account. Later, when I was a bit older, we would use the money I made to pay for my dance classes, singing lessons, and costumes. Even as a tiny tot, I was already putting my money right back into the business, a tactic I still employ.

I loved going on auditions back then, because it was like putting on shows. Even when I was just at home, I was always bouncing around the house, pretending I was performing. Renee knew she needed to do something to get all of this energy and creativity out of me, so I wouldn't drive her crazy. She enrolled me in ballet and tap at Art Linkletter Studio.

I still remember my first tap number, which was to a song called "Mississippi Mud." I wore a gold and black leotard with bows on it. My hat looked like a pie plate. The teacher told us that we all had to spray silver paint on our tap shoes for our costume. I won the Personality Award at the recital. I don't know if I had a good or bad personality, but I sure had a *lot* of it.

I loved being in dance class so much that Renee started putting me in children's theater. I joined both the Children's Civic Theater, which did seasonal theater productions, and the Atlanta Workshop Players, which would do monthly cabaret shows. Those were a combination of song, dance, variety, comedy, sketches, and everything else they could dream up for us kids. My grandmother was an excellent seamstress and would sometimes make my costumes for period pieces. I still have some of them.

The Children's Civic Theater would stage its shows at the Peachtree Theater, which is now a nightclub called Opera. These days, when I hit the club in Atlanta, I can see the spot where I stood on stage during all those productions.

As I got a bit older, I started to take performing even more seriously. I took voice lessons as well as dance classes. I changed to Fleetwood Studios and joined their travel team, which would compete against other studios. We weren't the best, we weren't the worst, but we were very dedicated.

I had a friend named Kim who was in the Atlanta Workshop Players with me, and she danced at Fleetwood Studios as well. We would perform duets together in the company. Eventually, in high school, she left to go study ballet with some incredible Russian teacher and our paths split.

In the meantime, we would go to performance-based summer camp. We'd spend a week in a cabin in northern Georgia out in the woods working on a number or two. At the end of the week, everyone's parents would come pick them up and we'd give a recital. It was kind of like *Dirty Dancing* minus the dramatic lift in the final scene—no Patrick Swayzes here!

At around ten, I was part of a pilot called *The River Ratz Club*. It was a scripted kids' show with songs and music. It was in the same vein as *Kids Incorporated*, the show where Fergie got her start. Our kids were a bit more country. We were hanging around with animals and stuff like that. We only made one episode, and it never went anywhere, but my mother still kept the folder from when I did it. She gave it to me recently, along with a box of other mementos. It's thirty years later, but if they want to go to series, I still have the original script! Thanks, Renee, for sacrificing your basement all those years.

A lot of little girls like to dance and perform, but for me it was slightly different. I didn't have brothers and sisters, and my mom was single for most of my childhood. My grandmother helped out a lot, but it was also important that I had somewhere to go. I think that's the biggest gift my family gave me, through my mom's divorces and the other tumultuousness of my childhood. I always had something to enjoy in my life, and that was the performing arts.

I met my friends through performing. I was also exposed to the LGBTQ community, people who were different from me. The thing about the arts and being around creative people is that there is less discrimination over color, race, sexual orientation, or creed. It's just about talent. People only cared if you had it or not. If you were the best dancer, you got the part. It didn't matter what color your skin was, or how much money your family had, or whether you were raised by a single mother.

At my elementary school in Lilburn, Georgia, I would always perform in the talent show. In fourth grade, I sang Dolly Parton's "9 to 5." I wore a purple satin jumper with silver sequins that my grandmother made for me. My blond hair was swept back in Farrah Fawcett wings, with a big lavender feather sticking out. It was somewhat redneck, but also totally adorable. This was the first of many manifestations of my love affair with Dolly Parton.

By the time I entered sixth grade, Renee had appointed herself my "creative director." She has always been what I would call a square. Her taste is much more toward the classics and I was always oriented toward pop culture. I wanted to sing something that was on the radio, but Renee forced me to do "My Favorite Things" from *The Sound of Music* in my fifth-grade talent show. My grandmother made me a beautiful smocked dress for the occasion. But even a good outfit can't save a boring number.

When I was a child, my mother married my stepfather twice. The first time was when I was three and the second time was when I was eight. They divorced for the second and final time when I was twelve. Soon before their second divorce, my mother and stepfather took a trip to Vegas. They saw a show at the Stardust called *Le Lido de Paris* and I later found the program. (I would eventually film my very first video as Erika Jayne on that same stage at the Stardust.) It featured these beautiful women with glittering, barely there costumes and huge feather headdresses. *Oh my God*, I thought, *this is what I want to be doing.* I never wanted to sing like Julie Andrews, but I absolutely wanted to be out there with a big costume wowing the crowd.

Although we lived in the conservative South, no one in my family ever blanched at stage nudity. I think it's because my mother and grandmother were both artists. They recognized those women were professionals plying a craft. Staying that fit and performing in those costumes every night was a difficult job.

When I was in eighth grade, I went to go see Madonna's Virgin tour when it came to Atlanta. That really changed my life. Because they had an extra ticket, I was able to go with my friend Kim from dance class and her older sister Julie.

I thought, *This woman is marrying elements of musical theater with pop music. Look at these cool costumes and these songs.* That's when I realized this was my lane. I didn't want to do "My Favorite Things." I wanted to be like Madonna.

As much fun as I was having with the kids in dance class and community theater, I wasn't really loving life at the Catholic school my mother and stepfather sent me to. My classmates thought I was stuck up and arrogant because I would go off to do plays, commercials, and dance recitals. All the other kids were really into sports, and they didn't understand what I was into. We were twelve years old, so they made fun of anything that made me stand out from the pack—and they chose this.

Of course I wanted to be accepted, but this is the age where kids begin pulling away from each other. You can start to see what kind of adults they are going to become. I realized that the kids at Catholic school would never be part of my tribe.

Most of them were headed down a much more traditional path toward conventional careers. That never held any appeal for me, so I veered a different way.

When it came time to attend high school, Renee and I moved out of my grandparents' house in Decatur, Georgia. We had moved there when my stepfather left for the second and final time, because it had broken my mother financially. Once she got her life back together, she bought a condo in Atlanta, and we came roaring back to the city.

This meant I could attend Northside High School, a public school that had a magnet program for the performing arts. Thank God she had split from my stepfather. If she hadn't, I probably would have been forced to go to a Catholic high school, which wouldn't have been good for me. To get into Northside's magnet program, I had to audition. I don't remember what song I sang, but it was good enough to get me into the Musical Theater Department. I'm thankful for that.

Just like every other high school kid, I had to take algebra, English literature, chemistry, biology, and the rest of it. But then two hours of my day were spent working in the Musical Theater Department.

Some kids came for art, drama, dance, or other disciplines. The Theater Tech Department (where I met my first boyfriend,

Jonathan) created all the lighting and sets for our productions. The school's orchestra would perform for our musicals.

Starting my sophomore year, I was also in the school's "tour show." Every year, we would put on a review and perform around the world. About thirty kids traveled, chaperoned by Mr. Densmore, the head of the Musical Theater Department. He was in his fifties, tall, with a bald head surrounded by a horseshoe of gray curls. He looked exactly like how you'd imagine a high school music teacher. He was great at his job, taking the kids seriously and cultivating their talent. Mr. Densmore was always working to bring more visibility and cachet to our program. He was hard on me, but to be fair he was hard on all of us. He certainly didn't have an easy job. Dealing with thirty unruly high school kids is hard enough, but add to it all of these creative kids with their egos and insecurities. Hopefully, Mr. Densmore had a lifetime supply of Xanax to get him through those trips.

Kids in the arts grow up fast. There's a certain level of maturity that comes from having to be responsible for being at rehearsal on time, learning all your lines, taking care of your costume, doing your own hair and makeup, not missing the call time, and doing a good job on stage. Anyone who didn't do all those things wouldn't last very long.

Don't get me wrong—especially in the later years in Europe, we were sneaking out at night to hit up the clubs and drink. It was legal at eighteen there, and we were all having a great time. We socialized like adults, trying to act more mature than we actually were. For all intents and purposes, we were adults. Adults with no bills, which is the best kind to be.

Every spring break, all of the arts kids would travel to a different city in Europe, while all of our other schoolmates were being rednecks at Panama City Beach in Florida. We would go to different churches in Brussels, London, Paris, or Vienna. The orchestra would play and all of the musical students would sing Latin mass. Tour show would also play theater dates for the local audiences. We got to travel and see the world while working on our craft, which is far better than wasting our spring break sitting on the sofa watching *The Price Is Right*.

Each year, the tour show had a different theme. One year it was a salute to Broadway, another year it was pop hits, things like that. We did both standards from the songbook and contemporary hits from the eighties. My junior year was a banner one, because I got to reprise my role as Dolly Parton singing "9 to 5." That same year, I was also cast as Madonna, and did "Into the Groove." I wore black patent leather booties, black lace tights under a black skirt, and a black Betsey Johnson top that was shaped almost like an inverted triangle. I wore a black lace bow in my hair, and of course black lace gloves. You can't do early Madonna realness without black lace gloves. I thought I was so cool, I was practically on that Virgin tour.

Most people in the show got a solo number, but it was a ninety-minute performance, with about fifteen numbers. So when you weren't in the spotlight, you were singing and dancing backup for someone else or backstage getting into another costume for the next number. Everyone wanted to be in every number and to be out on that stage as much as possible. (Thirty years later and it's just like some of those Real Housewives fighting for camera time.)

Travis Payne, who would play a pivotal role later in my life, was one of my good friends in tour show. All of my friends at Northside High School were in the arts programs there; the "normal" kids in our algebra and economics classes weren't part of our circle.

Occasionally, tour show would make additional trips abroad. When Atlanta was wooing the Olympic host committee to hold the Summer Games there, we flew to Tokyo to represent our city. Throughout the school year, we would perform all around the Atlanta region.

Coca-Cola, which is headquartered in Atlanta, sponsored our school, so we got to do some really cool stuff thanks to that affiliation. In 1987, for the celebration of Atlanta's 150th birthday celebration, the company put on a huge performance at the Coliseum (which is now Philips Arena). It told the history of the brand through song and dance. Yes, it sounds like a cheesy half-time show, but it was really spectacular. They laid out a lot of dough for this thing with sets, costumes, and lights. They also hired Michael Peters, who had choreographed Michael Jackson's iconic "Thriller" and "Beat It" videos, to do the choreography.

Peters brought in dancers from Los Angeles to be the featured performers, but they took the best from the dance and musical theater departments at Northside High to back them up. We had all been in shows before, obviously, but this was the first time any of us were seeing a real production with a big bankroll behind it. At the time, working with Michael fucking Peters was just about the coolest thing a dance kid could imagine.

In addition to having a touring show that performed at home and abroad, we would also regularly stage musicals locally. We performed them at the Woodruff Arts Center, a huge complex in Atlanta. I was a natural as Val in *A Chorus Line*, and I still remember all the words from her signature song, "Tits and Ass." (It was very on brand for Erika Jayne, even before she existed.)

By the time my senior year rolled around, I was over high

school theater. I had already decided that I was moving to New York to start my career and had mentally checked out. There was a lot of internal politics about who got cast and what roles they would have, and I was tired of playing that particular game.

One thing about me is that when I've had it, I have had it. It's over. Mentally, I was planning the next step in my life. I didn't audition for the spring musical, which that year was *Pippin*. Well, Mr. Densmore decided to call Renee.

"Why hasn't Erika tried out for the spring musical?" he asked her.

"Listen, Billy," Renee said, since they were on a first-name basis. "I can't force this girl. She decided she didn't want to audition, and she's not going to." My mother often called me unruly, but at the end of the day she always had my back.

"The girl I cast in the role of Fastrada isn't working out, and I'm going to cast Erika in the role instead," he said. "You know that I can hold her diploma if she doesn't do this part for me?"

"I didn't know that, but I'll be sure to tell Erika," she replied.

If musicals aren't your thing, or you have never had a child in a musical theater program anywhere in the country (because they all do *Pippin*), Fastrada is the wife of Pippin's father, King Charlemagne. She has a creepy, somewhat incestuous relationship with her son, Louis. Fastrada gets one solo at the end of the first act in a song called "Spread a Little Sunshine." It's a cute waltz of a song, but the double entendres definitely hint that the sunshine she spreads beams out from between her legs. Even before I could legally vote, I was already being typecast as a temptress.

Being cast against my will just made me mad. I hadn't even auditioned, and I was forced to take this part. That meant rehearsals and everything else I didn't want to be doing. With Mr. Densmore and my mother both breathing down my neck, I decided I would give in. I had worked hard for that diploma. If playing the sexpot in the most seventies musical imaginable was what it would take to graduate, I would have to do it.

Then, after pulling this stunt with my mother, Mr. Densmore wouldn't get rid of the original girl in the part—he made us split it. There were four performances. She got opening night and the third night, I got the second night and closing night. Since we had the same size feet, I even had to lend her my shoes, which were the boxy high heels that every actress wears on Broadway. When I wasn't performing as Fastrada, I was in the chorus in the opening and closing numbers.

I wasn't thrilled about any of this, but I was going along with it to keep the peace and graduate. During the cast meeting for the third performance, Mr. Densmore told the cast that the other girl was going to be playing Fastrada in the third perfor-mance as planned *and* on closing night, which was supposed to be my night. He was just using me to scare the girl he had cast in the first place to bring her A game. I was his insurance policy. Now that he didn't need me, I was getting sidelined in a musical I didn't even want to be in!

That was the final straw. I played it cool and waited until everyone was in costume. I even put on my own opening num-ber costume, a gold lamé bandeau top and a gold lamé skirt slit up to my hip. I pretended like everything was fine. Right before the curtain went up, the lights dimmed in the theater. Every-one was taking their place on the stage, but I turned, pushed the backstage door open, walked out, got in my car, and drove off—in costume, looking fabulous. I didn't perform that third night or come back on the fourth night. I'm sure my sudden departure screwed up the spacing in the chorus, and no one on stage was quite sure what to do when there was no one to deliver my scant few lines. Too bad.

Mr. Densmore had already threatened to withhold my diploma and gotten Renee all panicked, and now he's going to take my closing night? If he wouldn't hold up his end of the bargain, why should I hold up mine? Like I said, when I'm done, I'm done.

You want to know the worst thing? That girl still has my shoes! These specific shoes were rather expensive, and I had only worn them once. She never gave them back. It's been decades, and I'm still mad about those shoes.

I did receive my diploma. That's all that really mattered to me. I also learned that I was never again going to let people hold power over me. I was so mad that I had to compromise for this man. I hated that he was in a position to hold something over my head.

Mr. Densmore died years ago. He was important to my education and my career, and I still regret not talking it out as adults and making peace with him. I haven't been back to Northside since I graduated. As corny as it sounds, I still have dreams that take place in the musical theater room. I spent four years there, which seemed like an eternity at the time. It was a big U-shaped room with three-tiered elevated seating, so the chorus could sing on risers. Mr. Densmore played his grand piano in the center.

In my dreams, I'm sitting in this room, talking to my friends seated all around me. It's almost like I'm reliving rehearsals for shows. It sounds so crazy, but it's like I'm catching up with my friends as though we never left. As if we could get up and break out singing "One" from *A Chorus Line*, in perfect unison and hitting every note and remembering every step. I'm fifteen again, and we're all coming in and out and moving around the room. I don't have that nightmare some people have, where I'm performing and haven't rehearsed. My dream *is* the rehearsal. That is where I'm at my happiest, working with the people I love and who can relate to me. Getting ready to do my favorite thing in the whole world, which is putting on a show.

2

CLASSIC RENEE

*M*y mother named me Erika, after her favorite soap opera character, Erica Kane on *All My Children*, played by Susan Lucci. When I was born she was eighteen and living in Atlanta, Georgia. She says that Erica Kane was everything that she wanted to be at the time: a smart, independent businesswoman. And a brunette.

My mother's name is Renee. My middle name, Nay, is based on "Nay-Nay." Allegedly, that's what my father used to call my mother as a pet name for Renee. I never tell anyone my middle name, because I hate it. It makes me sound so incredibly country. It also reminds me of my father. He married my mother when they found out she was pregnant, but then he left nine months after I was born. He was never a part of my life.

I always called my mom Renee because I felt like I was on a level playing field with her. It was never meant as a sign of disrespect not to call her Mom (which I still did occasionally). It was a reflection of the way I viewed our relationship. It was like in a past life we were friends, and somehow we ended up coming back as a mother and daughter. I wasn't going to call a peer Mom.

Just like my relationship with my middle name, my relationship with my mother has been complicated. She's been one of the closest people in my life, but no one can infuriate me the way she does.

I think I came along at a very difficult time for my mother. She was a natural blonde with a perfect bombshell body. She was eighteen and seeking magic. Instead, she ended up with a young child, a husband who took off, and a lot of difficulties. She dreamed of a future as a painter and concert pianist. Despite being artistic enough to succeed at either, instead she ended up as a bank teller who taught piano on the side. This was the South in the early seventies which was still very conservative and not forward thinking. After having a child and a failed marriage so young, she was just considered finished.

Renee always had a level of anxiety, which was often related to bills. She worried about having enough money for the both of us. She didn't have the kind of freedom or career she dreamed about when she was young. I bore the brunt of a lot of that stress. She was short with me, hard on me, and irritable. She would snatch my ponytail, dig her nails into my arm, and step on my feet. And that was in public. At home she got me with the belt. She was never a lot of fun to be around. In short, she could be a real ass.

The thing I heard her say more than anything else was, "I'm miserable." And it showed. I don't really remember my mother smiling or laughing a lot. I don't remember much joy there. She was disappointed and angry, and I think we would both agree that I got the brunt of it.

Now that I'm older, I can recognize that I always had a high level of anxiety as a child. Because of my mother's situation, I never knew when the bottom might fall out. I took on the role of thinking, *Oh my God, are we going to get kicked out of this house because we can't afford it? What if she loses her job? What will we do then?*

It was just the two of us. I was a child and totally focused on her. When she was a wreck, it affected me, too. I felt isolated, with no one to turn to, play with, or talk to. It takes a toll in stressful times when you have no one to lean on. My grandparents were a stable influence, but we didn't live with them all the time. Imagine the anxiety of seeing the one and only person who can take care of you upset and crying because you don't have enough money.

Renee is also incredibly indecisive. "Well, I don't really know," she would drawl whenever I asked her what we were going to do. This would be about everything, from the major stuff, like moving to New York, to the minor things, like what she wanted to do that weekend. She always seemed rudderless. To this day, ordering a meal with her drives me crazy.

"Well, I don't really know whether to have the steak or the pasta," she'll tell the waiter.

I want to scream at her, "Just pick one, Renee! It's one meal. We'll have thousands more in our lifetime. Just make up your mind."

She treated me like an adult when she really shouldn't have. I think she expected me to understand or process certain situations in a more adult manner than I was able to—especially when it came to work and money. There's a fine line between keeping kids totally in the dark and telling them the adult truth. I don't think she got that balance right, and she erred on the side of telling me more than I could handle. Because she was under tremendous pressure, I think she collapsed slightly in on herself. She had a hard time finding her strength. It was almost like she needed me to get us both through the tough times.

Being with that kind of mother made me grow up very fast. She always made me shake people's hands and look at them in the eye, even as a kid. I was expected to act and present myself like a miniadult rather than a young child.

When I was small and working with a talent agency, she would make me call the agent and book all of my own appointments. That also meant that I got to show up and pick up my own checks at the agency. Eventually, I was doing it all myself. Partly it's because Renee didn't have time. But she also gave me the same work ethic she inherited from my grandparents.

My mother was raised by Depression-era parents. They taught her—and me—that the world is difficult and often disappointing. We were told that life is hard. It is always going to be difficult, but if you work hard enough, you can have something—but probably not, so don't get too disappointed. It was almost as if they were instilling in us the sense to stay in our place. We could dream—but not too much.

I was motivated as a child, but not by positive circumstances. I wasn't aspiring to good things as much as I was trying to avoid the negative consequences of *not* doing something.

When I was little, my grandparents owned a lake house not far from where we lived. They had a powerboat that we would take out for waterskiing. I loved being in the water, and I was athletic as a kid. But when I was learning, I had a hard time getting out of the water and up on the skis. My mother was frustrated that I wasn't getting it. Finally, she told me that I had to get up on my skis because there was a water moccasin in the lake. Right quick, I figured out how to get up on those skis. That little fib did the trick. But from then on, I was always worried that the lake was full of snakes.

My grandfather, Hollis, was the best speedboat driver. He'd have some shots of Wild Turkey and a few beers, then he'd just whip me around that lake. Eventually I got so good I would put on my ski and jump directly from the dock. I would never even have to get in the lake. Because, you know, snakes.

Renee's influence on my performing career was equally complicated. On the one hand, she always made sure that we had enough money for dance lessons, costumes, and anything else I might need for the children's theater productions I was in. She made sure that I got rides to and from all of those things, and that I had all the tools necessary to succeed. I will always be grateful that she taught me that I could do anything I wanted to do.

On the other hand, she could be incredibly cruel. In middle school, I was in dress rehearsal for a production of *The Wiz.* Or maybe it was *The Wizard of Oz,* but had songs in it? I don't remember, but I do remember standing at the front of the stage in my costume, a light blue jumper. I was going over my solo for the show. Renee was sitting in the audience. This particular song sat in the break of my voice, the middle register where I have a hard time singing. It was challenging to seamlessly blend a heavier chest tone into a lighter, airier head tone. When I was getting to the high note, I switched into a falsetto voice to hit the note, and I heard Renee's laugh echoing around the room. I stopped singing immediately.

Yes, it was a struggle, but I had hit the note. Instead of trying to help me or be encouraging, Renee often laughed at me. There was always a dagger in her comments about a performance I gave. She would say, "That could have been better," or, "I didn't like that." She ripped me to shreds all the time, but this was the first time that she ever did it in front of other people. To this day, whenever I'm on stage or in the recording booth, I'm constantly paranoid about being on key. I'm always visualizing the constant criticism from Renee.

That's what was so odd about her. She would enable me to perform in this show, but then she would tear me down as I did it. She would never miss a performance, but if I did something she didn't like, she'd say, "That's stupid, why did you do that?" It was a total mindfuck.

When I was in the Musical Theater Department at Northside High School, we were doing a talent showcase where students could select any number they wanted. It was like the sort of talent shows other high schools would have, which was unusual for us because we were accustomed to more structured performances. Renee got wind of this performance and put her two cents in, acting as my creative director one more time. She was convinced I should perform a song from *The Phantom of the Opera*.

"I shouldn't do that song for two reasons," I explained. "First, there's a really high part that's not a fit for my voice. Second, it's not going to be that kind of night. I think I need to do something with a much more pop feel." I knew that I was going to get buried because the other students were going to do cool stuff, nothing as corny and stiff as *The Phantom of the Opera*.

Renee was relentless. She badgered me until I finally gave up and sang the piece she selected just to keep her happy. The night of the show, she came with her girlfriend. From the stage, I could see exactly where she was sitting in the audience. I got on stage wearing silver lamé pants and a matching top, with big shoulder pads and my hair to one side. I was trying to add a little sparkle to this number.

As I predicted, I gave a very average performance of the song. The response from the crowd was tepid at best. I could see my mother and her friend making faces while I tried to get through a number I didn't even want to do.

I walked off stage where my classmate Mildred, who sang

"And I'm Telling You I'm Not Going" in that year's tour show production, was sitting on some sound equipment with her feet dangling over the edge. As I walked by, she shook her head and said, "Man, that was fucked up."

"Yeah, I know. Thanks," I said.

After the show, I pointed out to my mother that my number hadn't gone very well. "Yeah," she said. "While you were singing it, I was sliding down in my seat."

My mother was so young when she had me, and my grandmother—her mother—was such a maternal figure in my life that Renee and I could behave more like competitive sisters than mother and daughter.

My junior year in high school, I had a solo in Northside's tour show. I sang "9 to 5" and dressed like Dolly Parton. That Halloween, I went ice skating at an indoor rink with my boyfriend and his family. I took a freak fall and slammed the back of my head on the ice and passed out. My boyfriend's father was a doctor at Piedmont Hospital, and he was worried I might have a concussion. They put me in the back of their van and drove me to the hospital.

When I got to the hospital, someone called my mother. I was having a hard time staying awake. I was really out of it. When they asked me to touch my nose with my right hand, I touched my left ear. I got out of the MRI and my mother was there. She was wearing my Dolly Parton costume from the tour show. She had on the big platinum wig, the denim shirt that ties in the front, the skintight jeans, cowboy boots, everything—including my fake giant Dolly Parton triple Ds. I was lying there with the neurologist when she walked in with her friend Cheryl who was dressed as Reba McIntyre. I slurred, "Are you wearing my Dolly Parton costume?"

"Yes," Renee said. "We went out to the club for Halloween, and I needed a costume." I was so embarrassed. Here I was with a head injury bad enough to keep me in the hospital for several days, and my mother showed up in my costume with her best friend looking like they were about to go on stage at the Grand Ole Opry.

The neurologist was checking my brain functions and he told me to count down from a hundred, subtracting seven each time. I said, "Ninety-three. Uhhhhh . . ." and blanked on the next number.

"What's seven from that?" the doctor asked.

"Shit, she can't do that when she's normal," Renee said. "She's not good in math." I started to wish she hadn't come to the hospital at all.

Just like almost every teenage girl and her mother, we used to fight. With Renee, things could get really bad. She would sometimes say the most hateful things to me. Once, in the middle of some fight (probably over something stupid), it got so heated she said to me, "I wish that I never had you."

That stung so badly. In part, because I knew it was true. People can feel when they're unwanted. I know Renee loved me, but I knew she would have been okay without me. She probably would have preferred to follow her dreams rather than having to raise me.

I definitely picked up Renee's talent for saying hateful things, and I would use it against her. That's why I'm always so afraid to lose my temper on *The Real Housewives of Beverly Hills*. If I ever did, I'm afraid I would really eviscerate someone.

I would cuss her out every now and again, but I was basically a good kid. I played by the rules, took care of myself, and did not get in trouble, but I didn't have a lot of respect for my mother.

That's not to say that everything was horrible, and I know there are people who had it worse. She wasn't a drug addict; she never beat me or neglected me. But there was a sense of stability and guidance I wanted from my mother that I never got. I had to develop that on my own.

I have to hand it to her, though—when I needed it, Renee always had my back. There would be moments when she would be so clutch. One example is the summer before my senior year. Because I was in the musical theater program at Northside High

School, there wasn't time for me to take my economics and health classes during the school year. I had to make them up at summer school. Instead of being at Northside, these classes were at Harper High School. One day after class, I found a note on the windshield of my car.

"You don't belong here," it read. "If you keep coming here, we're going to beat the shit out of you." I got home and showed the note to Renee. I was a little concerned about my safety, but mostly I was worried about whether I would be able to finish summer school. I needed those credits to graduate on time.

The next day, Renee marched down to the school. She barged into the principal's office and demanded a meeting with him. She showed him the note and said, "What are you going to do about this? I'm not going to have my daughter feel unsafe at your school." I don't know if it was Renee's presence or tone or what, but after that, I never had any trouble. The situation got handled.

When I was in middle school we lived in a two-story house in Lilburn, Georgia. On weekend mornings, Renee would play classical music at the upright piano in our living room. It was usually reserved for her piano students, but sometimes she'd make an exception. She'd play for hours, the notes drifting up to my room as I would lie in bed and listen. I was scared that if I got up, the music might stop.

At my house now we have a Steinway grand piano. Whenever Renee comes to visit, I love it when she plays for me. It reminds me of all of those mornings when things seemed peaceful and beautiful, even if just for a short time.

I think when I went to Los Angeles at twenty-five and moved away from her completely it was the best thing that ever happened to us. I needed to be my own woman. I think she needed to be on her own, too. To focus on herself and not have to worry about me.

Now I can finally have a good time with my mother. She's a lot more fun when she's not stressed out about money and raising a kid. We actually have a fair amount in common. We're both artistic and creative, very ambitious, and we both know how to work hard.

Renee is much happier with her life now than she was when I was younger. After working as a bank teller when I was very small, she continued working in the mortgage industry. She was good at it and made great money, but it was never her passion.

In 2008, the mortgage industry blew up. I told her, "This is the best thing to ever happen to you. Now you can do what you really want to do." She went back to school at Georgia State and got her bachelor's degree in fine arts. The moment she got on that path, she became a much freer, nicer person.

When her parents got sick—my grandfather with cancer

and my grandmother with Alzheimer's—she moved into their house to help take care of them. She would have to commute to downtown Atlanta every day for school, but *still* managed to make the dean's list! It was a hard time for her, but like I said, no one is finer in the clutch than Renee. While she was in school, I would send her on a painting trip each summer so she could have a break from school and her parents. She had really earned some time alone.

When my grandparents died, she stayed in their house. Recently, she decided to put the house on the market. "When this house goes, that's the last of my parents," she told me.

"But this house was *their* dream," I told her. "It was never your dream. It was their life. You're in your sixties. You should go have your own life. You need to do what makes you happy. You need to go where you need to be."

"That's true," she said.

"So what do you want to do now?" I asked.

She said, "Well, I don't really know . . ."

Classic Renee.

3

FATHER FIGURES

One of my very first memories is from my third birthday party. I was at my maternal grandparents' house, and my grandmother Ann was holding me in her arms. "Oh look," she said in an excited, high-pitched voice. "There is your grandfather!"

"Who?" I asked. I did not understand that I had another grandfather other than her husband, my grandfather Hollis, in whose house I was living at the time. She meant my father's father. I had never met my other grandfather before. But then again, I hadn't ever met my father, either.

I was looking out of the large plate glass windows that overlooked her beautiful garden in the backyard. My birthday is in July, so the garden was lush in the summer sun. The memory is just a blurry flash. I don't even remember meeting him, just being told that my grandfather was present.

I'm told that my paternal grandfather was a very tall man and that he gave me a little carousel as a gift that day. My mother said that I loved it, and for a while it was my favorite toy. That was the only time he visited. He and my grandmother Ann were in contact, and that's how she'd invited him to come to my birthday party. When I was older, she told me that she used to mail him pictures of me. She hoped he would pass them on to my father, but instead he would just return them. Eventually, when I was in middle school, he sent her a note asking her to stop sending the pictures altogether.

My paternal grandfather grew up in northern Georgia and joined the military, where, according to family legend, he served as Dwight Eisenhower's personal assistant. When in Miami, he met Esther, a small Mayan woman. She'd inherited a coffee plantation in El Salvador called Esperanza after her first husband died. My grandfather married her and moved to El Salvador, where he helped expand the plantation and raise the children from her first marriage. They had three sons together, my father, Nicolas, being the oldest.

The way the story was told to me, the communists were rampaging through their country and seized my grandmother's plantation. In the middle of the night, my grandfather got his three boys and ran through the jungle to get them on a plane going back to the United States. He left my grandmother there with her three older children. He had been in the military, so he knew things were only going to get worse, and he only took care of himself and his sons. The four of them resettled back in Atlanta when my father was fifteen, his brother Gabriel was fourteen, and the youngest, Alejandro, was three. They moved into a house on Don Juan Lane in Decatur, Georgia. I'm not kidding. I can't make this shit up. It was like they moved to Latin Lover Lane.

I only met my paternal grandmother Esther once, even though she sent me Christmas cards in Spanish for years. She wore a floor-length chinchilla coat and carried a cigarette holder. She was known to get her hair and makeup done every day. She was very grand. She came to my grandmother Ann's house and gave me one of those dolls that pees when you feed it a baby bottle and whose diaper you can change. She didn't speak English, but she told me the doll's name was Lolita. After he took off with their children in the middle of the night, Esther never got back together with my grandfather. I don't think she ever forgave him for taking her children away, especially Alejandro, being only three.

These kids—now teenagers—who had grown up in El Salvador, were wild. My grandfather, a former military man, couldn't handle living in a house with three messy, unruly boys. He built them a shed behind his house where they could live and run wild. He let Alejandro live inside the house, though.

All three boys spoke Spanish and English with perfect accents. They were all devastatingly handsome and had that Latin bad boy air of not giving a shit. My father and his brother Gabriel carried sawed-off shotguns in their cars and weren't afraid to let everyone know it. This attitude made them absolutely irresistible to all the girls in their high school. My mom sure found it sexy.

Renee was friendly with my father's younger brother Gabriel. He invited her to go to a party with him. Even though he had just broken up with his girlfriend, Renee insists that it wasn't a date. At that party, he introduced her to the man who would become my father, and the two of them started dancing together. "When are you going to ask me out?" Renee said, and he did so on the spot. It's funny, because years later, when I was working as a cocktail waitress at Chasen's, I used a similar trick to get Tom Girardi—my future husband—to ask me out.

They dated for a few months and fell in love. When Renee became pregnant, they got married. It only lasted eighteen months, and Nicolas divorced my mother when I was nine months old.

Everyone in my family always liked my dad and said nice things about him, but I think two things were happening here. Number one, my mother was eighteen years old and he was twenty-three. They were both young, and there is a lot of drama and immaturity that goes along with that.

Number two, I think my grandmother Ann was probably really overbearing and tried to control everything, because that's who she was. My mother and father lived right next door to her, so they never had the chance to be grown-ups on their own. That couldn't have been easy for them.

Just recently, my mother told me that after she and my father separated, she moved back in with her parents. One day, my father called and asked to take her out. My grandparents babysat me while my parents went to the drive-in in the black Dodge Charger he bought brand-new when I was born.

On their date, my father said to Renee, "Tomorrow I'm going to come by your parents' house, pick you up, and we're going to go hunt for apartments. The three of us will live together and be a little family." It was really romantic at the drive-in, so this was all fabulous.

He dropped her off at my grandparents' house. The next day, my mother waited and waited. He never came. He never called. Finally, she called her friend Janet, who had recently married Nicolas's brother Gabriel. She asked if Janet had seen my father. "Oh no, honey, he's moved to California. He left this morning," Janet said.

When she told me the story, my mother said, "Erika, he had it all planned out. As we were making out in the car at the drive-in, I was wondering why all of his clothes were hanging on a rod in the backseat."

I don't think my father wanted to be a dad. He was a mechanic at a car dealership in town at that time and he wanted a different life for himself. Once he moved to California, my father wasn't a part of my life at all. I vaguely remember him coming by my grandmother's house to see me one time when I was very young. But it's more like I recall his presence rather than actually seeing him or spending time with him. That's it.

But that doesn't mean his family wasn't around. My mother was very close with my aunt Janet and still is to this day. She even went as Erika Jayne one year for Halloween. I remember when I was very small, before kindergarten, going over a couple of times to the house she shared with my uncle.

Janet eventually divorced my uncle for what my mother considered more than sufficient cause. He moved in with his brother Alejandro in an apartment complex.

Janet moved to an apartment and started a new job as a beautician when she left my uncle. She drove a silver Corvette that she absolutely loved. A week after she moved, she came out of her apartment to go to work but couldn't see her car anywhere in the parking lot. What did she see in her parking space? A big black hearse with a manila envelope taped to the windshield with the word JANET printed on it.

My uncle had taken her car and left a hearse in its place. She had just started this job, so she couldn't be late for work. She decided to drive the hearse and deal with it later. The worst part was, when she got in and started the car with the keys that were in the ignition, it only went in reverse. She was totally stranded. To this day, no one has figured out how my uncle had gotten this busted-ass car there in the first place.

The whole situation—between her and my uncle, between my mom and my dad—was just a southern-style shambles.

After my father left, Renee never really dated. I mean, if she dated, she did it on the down low. She never had anyone over at the house spending the night. My mother was very conscientious about that. She didn't have boyfriends. She didn't try to pawn me off on someone else. She wasn't that mom.

When I was three, she married my stepfather, John. My mother tells me that I was in the wedding, but I have zero recollection of that. Probably because I knew their relationship was bullshit, even at three years old. From the beginning the strain between them was obvious, and I had enough of a feel for my mother to know that this would never last.

My first memory of them as a couple is when they were off at Disneyland for their honeymoon. My grandmother watched me, because we were living with her then. I was sitting on my grandmother's white leather couch when she came over and said to me, "Now that your mom got married, you're not going to be living here anymore."

My mom came back from vacation and we all moved into an apartment near my grandmother's house. Soon they bought a cute little ranch house in Stone Mountain, Georgia. We had a big backyard and it was very middle class.

My stepfather was handsome and tall, maybe six foot two. He was from Pittsburgh, from a nice family of Polish immigrants. Sometimes we would go to Pittsburgh, just the two of us, and we'd go ice skating and sledding and do the things we couldn't do down south.

He was always very loving and kind toward me. We played sports and bonded over baseball and cars. He was in the car business and would drag me around everywhere with him, even the auto auction. Later on, he owned a used-car lot, so he and Renee were always getting new cars and swapping out their old ones to sell. I knew all about cars, and I would always beg him to bring home the fastest one on the lot. He's the one who really started my lifelong love of fast cars.

I've always been afraid of the dark, so it was very hard for me to sleep as a child. I would try to sneak into my parents' bed and my mom would get mad. But my stepfather used to let me sneak in on his side and sleep next to him.

As sweet as he was with me, he and my mother had a rocky relationship. There was a lot of fighting and volatility. They were both under thirty, trying to hold down jobs, and raising a young daughter. Then my mother found out there was another woman in my stepfather's life and that was the end of their relationship.

Renee was working as a bank teller as well as teaching piano. One weekend, she went away on a painting trip to Edisto Beach, South Carolina. The weekend was a bit weird, because my stepfather was sleeping in the guest room. As usual, I fell asleep in my little bed and then went to crawl in with him in the middle of the night when I got scared of the dark.

I remember lying in bed with him, thinking, *Why are we in here? This is strange. I don't have any connection to this room at all.*

Suddenly I started to get mad at him, like I could intuit that something bad was going on between him and Renee. I was five and looking over at the bathroom, thinking, *I don't want to get up. I don't feel comfortable. So, I'm just gonna pee in this bed.*

That's what I did. I have never wet the bed before or since, but that one time I was a bed wetter—out of spite.

"Oh my God, Erika. What's wrong?" he asked, startled as he jumped out of bed.

"Oh, I don't know. I'm sorry. I just couldn't make it," I told him. But I was peeing on him on purpose. It's almost as if I knew what was coming, like, "Fuck you."

The next day, Renee returned from her trip and my stepfather packed his car and left. That was the reason we were sleeping in the guest room, because he had been packing up all of his things in their bedroom. At the time, I didn't know the details of what went wrong with his and Renee's relationship, just that she returned from her trip and the next day my stepfather packed up and left us. At the time, you could get a no-fault divorce in Georgia in thirty days, and a month later, the papers were signed. It was all over.

For the next year, there were no men in my mother's life. Then one day, she said to me, "He's moving back in." She meant my stepfather. Unbeknownst to me, the two of them had been talking on the phone regularly the entire year. They had reconciled while he was living back near his family in Pittsburgh. They decided to get married for a second time.

I still remember staring out the window of our ranch house, seeing his car pull up, and vibrating with excitement, thinking, *Oh my God, my stepfather's back. He's back.*

The thing about John is he was always great in business.

Very motivated. The one consistent thing in my life is that everyone around me has always been a hard worker. This includes both of my husbands, my stepfather, my father, my mother, my grandparents, and my son.

After a few years, we upgraded and bought a bigger house in Lilburn, Georgia. It was a big, two-story home. I transferred to Lilburn Elementary School and, for the first and only time in my life, brought home straight As. Renee was working with my stepfather, helping him run the car lot. It was just like how my grandmother had helped my grandfather run his plumbing company.

For a while, things were very good between Renee and my stepfather. My mother went so far as to apply for an annulment for her first marriage (to my father) so that she and my stepfather could get their union recognized by the Catholic church. When I was ten, Renee pushed to have my stepfather legally adopt me.

By that time, I think my stepfather considered me his child. I think he really did love me. This adoption push came in the summertime. I was upstairs in the house and my mother was sitting on her bed, talking on the phone.

"Your father wants to talk to you," she told me, holding out the receiver.

Huh? What? I thought, a bit confused to speak to this man I'd only heard about until now. "Okay."

I got on the phone with him, and he asked if I wanted my stepfather to adopt me. The whole thing was confusing to me, because I was just a kid. I knew this man on the phone was my "real" dad. I knew that my stepfather was doing this thing called adoption. But at age ten, I wasn't sure what all that meant. I just wanted to go to ballet class and be done with it.

"Is this something you want to do?" my father asked.

"Yeah," I said automatically. I didn't know what I wanted, but Renee really wanted it, and I wanted to make her happy.

Apparently, that was enough for my father. He relinquished his parental rights so my stepfather could legally adopt me. That summer, the process was completed and I got a brand-new birth certificate with my stepfather's last name as my last name.

We had a few great years together, with Renee and my stepfather getting along and the business thriving. But then the fighting resumed when Renee discovered that he'd been unfaithful again. One day when I was in middle school, it all blew up. He left us for the second (and what would be the final) time on Thanksgiving. That year, none of us had much to be thankful for.

By that point in their relationship, I was done with both of them. To be honest, I've been done with these people since I was basically walking and talking. I thought, *This is dumb, the whole thing is dumb. This is not going to work out.* It's crazy how instinctually right I was about their relationship. If I could see as a kid that it wasn't going to work out, why the hell couldn't they see it?

While they were fighting and cussing each other out, I didn't blame myself as some kids do. I didn't think there was anything wrong with me. I knew that everything was wrong with *them*. There are two things I knew since the day I was born: I was fine, and my grandmother and I were the only two sane motherfuckers out of all of these crazy people.

The day that my stepfather left was hard, though. Renee sat in a chair in the living room, wearing a pair of navy shorts and a purple polo shirt. She was sobbing into her hands. Her face was pressed into the side of the chair.

I thought—and I will never forget this—*I don't ever want to be like that.* I love my mother, but in that moment, I saw her as weak. I knew that she could survive without a man, but she wanted a partner so badly that she let him ruin her life. We'd had a great house. We'd had Christmas trees and parties and a yard and a dog named Cubby. It was all great. Now it was all gone.

Renee and I were still living in that big, two-story house.

But since she'd been working for his business, he was the one making all of the money. When he left, he cleaned out their checking account and left Renee with nothing. The next month, Renee didn't have enough money to pay the mortgage, keep the lights on, pay for her car, and buy Christmas presents.

I remember sitting at her piano, making up a song called "Slim Jim Christmas." "It's going to be a Slim Jim Christmas, everywhere you go," I sang as my mother played accompaniment. We had to laugh about the situation. We had to make fun of it, or else the gloom would have been too much to bear.

The irony is that my mother's annulment papers finally showed up in the mail the very next day after my stepfather left. She would finally be able to get married in the Catholic church! The only problem was that her husband was gone. I don't know if that's divine intervention, exactly, but it's *something*.

The second time the relationship ended wasn't as easy as the first time, back when my stepfather just took off and I didn't hear from him for a year. This time, he had adopted me. He had parental rights.

My mother and stepfather were trying to decide visitation. Because their divorce wasn't amicable, we all wound up in family court. I was about twelve and I was called in to testify about whether I wanted to see my stepfather or not. I had to go to court about three days in a row in the summertime in Lawrenceville, Georgia. I sat next to my grandmother on those hard wooden benches in that hot, stuffy courtroom. I just felt sick to my stomach the whole time. I kept asking my grandmother, "Can we leave now?" But no, we couldn't.

I heard too many adult things in that courtroom; hurtful, spiteful language. My mother was talking about what a bad husband my stepfather had been, and then he was saying the same sorts of things about my mother. It was all of that tit-for-tat bullshit.

I realize now it was not necessary to put a child in the middle of the divorce like that. Making a little girl sit on the stand and be questioned was cruel. I didn't want any part of it. Not on my mother's side and not on my stepfather's side. To this day, I don't appreciate it.

I was sick to my stomach with anxiety being in that courtroom. Decades later, when I first started to accompany my husband, Tom, to court, I would become nauseated. In the deep recesses of my brain, I always equate the courthouse with the awful feeling I had during those visitation disputes.

When it was all settled, I was scheduled to have visits with my stepfather. He had gotten an apartment, and I would go hang out with him there. We would go to the movies and stuff. It wasn't bad, it was just different. He was a good dad and never mean to me, so I'm not sure why I wanted to stop going to see him. There are some holes in my memory from back then, and this is one of them. Even Renee doesn't remember the specific reason.

When I told my mother that I no longer wanted to go, she asked her lawyer for advice. He said that the next time my step-father picked me up, I could go out in the driveway, look him in the eye, say, "I'm not coming," and then come back into the house. That was supposed to be good enough.

The next time he came for me, I saw his car pull up. I walked outside. My mother was at home, but she was upstairs putting on her makeup. She figured that I would deliver my lines as discussed, and everything would end peacefully. My grandmother Ann's sister, my great-aunt Helen, was standing by the window watching me walk out there to say I'm not coming. She had a feeling it wasn't going to be as easy as Renee assumed.

After I told him I didn't want to come, my stepfather got out of the car and tried to take me.

"Renee, he's got her!" Helen yelled to my mother. Helen and Renee came running out to stop him, and my mother tried to pull me away from him. My mother had one of my arms and my stepfather had the other; they were literally having a tug-of-war with me. I wrapped my feet around the railing leading up to the front porch and started crying. It was a spectacle, and all of the neighbors could see this scene unraveling in the front yard. It was just trashy.

My mother jumped onto my stepfather's back and started scratching him. Finally, he let me go. When he snatched me, it's like something in him had snapped. He was angry at my mother and wanted to see his little girl, and he was just enraged and frustrated. Finally he came back to his senses, and he dropped the whole thing. After that, I had to go see a child psychologist. Eventually, the court said that I no longer had to visit my stepfather if I didn't want to. I didn't see or speak to him again for a long time.

In fact, the next time I spoke to him was in 1989, just after my mother and I moved to New York. I was eighteen at the time, and my grandmother found out that my stepfather's parents were both killed in a tragic car accident. She was really good about reaching out to people in times of crisis. She called my stepfather's sister, who told my grandmother that when they went through her mother's possessions, my step-grandmother still had my picture in her wallet. As I reminisce on this story, I feel really terrible about that. There was so much sadness around that whole part of my life, and I wonder why she kept that photo all of those years.

After my grandmother told me that news, I thought I should reach out to my stepfather and give him my condolences. When he picked up the phone, I could hear noise in the background, like he had people over or there was a party going on.

I told him how sorry I was about his parents' death and asked him how he was doing, but he was hesitant to reply to me. I could almost feel him on the other end of the line, looking around the room and trying to find a way out of the conversation.

"Erika," he said finally. "I'd prefer if you didn't contact me again."

"Oh. Okay," I replied, a little stunned. "Take care."

That was the last time I ever spoke to him. I was sad that he wasn't happy to hear from me. Perhaps I was expecting too much, but looking back on it I think I understand why he felt that way. We'd always had a good relationship. I still think fondly of our time together, riding around in one of his many cars, going to a sporting event, or even just helping him run his errands around town. But he was already dealing with the heartache of his parents dying. The last thing he needed was this charged interaction on top of it.

I think his rejection had more to do with his relationship

with my mother. They still had hard feelings for each other. Hearing from me, I think, just reminded him of that pain. So I respected his wish and never called again.

As for Nicolas, my biological father, I never tried to contact him. My mother and grandmother would tell me stories to fill in the blanks. When I was being really bad, my mother would say, "Ugh, you're just like your father!" Which at that time meant nothing to me. I didn't feel the need to have a relationship with him. I had grown up very close to my grandfather Hollis, who is the one who would give me away at my first wedding. I'd also had a few good years with my stepfather. That was enough. I was satisfied.

My uncle Alejandro, however, had different ideas. Aunt Janet was long divorced from my uncle Gabriel, but she was still in touch with both my mother and Alejandro. He wanted things to be right between my father and me. He asked Janet if I would be interested in speaking with my father on the phone. Janet had my mother ask me, and I agreed. Through that complicated phone tree, we worked it out.

I was almost twenty-five. I had already been married and divorced and was living with my mother and five-year-old son in Tudor City in Manhattan. To be honest, that first phone call was a little awkward. I was talking to someone whom I had heard about for my entire life, someone who was obviously instrumental to my even being on this planet, but I really knew almost nothing about him. We played catch-up on our lives and talked about where we were and what we were doing.

I told him everything about myself. He confirmed that when he left Atlanta he moved to Oakland, California, and became a police officer. He was still working on the force. He was remarried and had a small daughter, who was younger than my son.

I was planning to visit Janet, who was living in West Hollywood by that time, in a few months. So my father and I arranged that when I got to the West Coast, I would meet him in person.

Janet lived right across the street from the Le Parc Hotel. It's a cool, rock 'n' roll hotel that has always been one of LA's hidden gems. He stayed at the hotel, and I walked across the street and met my father in his room. I always thought that I looked a lot like Renee, but as soon as I met him, I realized that it is my father who I really look like.

I have full lips and big, bushy eyebrows just like him. On my mother's side, I come from a long line of towheads with icy blue eyes. I'm the only one with green eyes, like my father. I'm also the only one with an ass. I have my father to thank (or maybe his mother) for giving me that blessing.

I shook his hand, and he gave me a bracelet. It was a big,

thick rope of gold. When I got back to New York, I immediately pawned it to some Hasidim in the Diamond District to pay the rent. They gave me around twelve hundred dollars, so I can only imagine how much it was really worth.

There wasn't that Hallmark movie moment where I saw him and shouted, "Oh, Daddy," and ran into his arms and we were suddenly the best of friends. There was none of that. It was very businesslike. What exactly do you say?

We went out for the day. I drove Janet's stick shift around town, and he told me, "You drive like a man." It's the only compliment my father ever gave me. I forget exactly what we were doing. No matter the activity, what we were *really* doing was feeling each other out. As sad as it sounds, we were just two strangers getting to know each other. This is when I learned about my grandparents and my father's childhood in El Salvador. I learned about the shed behind my grandfather's house and the unknown branches of my family tree.

At the end of our visit, he invited me to come stay with him and his family in the Bay Area for Thanksgiving, which I accepted. A few months later, I arrived. He picked me up from the airport, and I went to his townhouse outside Oakland. I met his wife, Bridget, who was very sweet, and his adorable young daughter, Fallon, who is my half sister.

"Let me show you what I do and show you around," he said.

We drove to the police station in downtown Oakland and he introduced me to his coworkers as his daughter. "Oh, that's funny," more than one person at the station said. "We've never heard of you before."

Then we went to the gun range, which is something all good southern dads do with their daughters. At twenty-five, I was finally getting my turn. At the shooting range he told me, "If I had raised you, you'd be walking around with a machine gun and a machete." Little did he know that I'd been shooting guns my whole life. My grandfather kept a double-barreled shotgun next to his bed and a machete under the driver's seat of his van. Atlanta and El Salvador weren't as far apart as he thought.

He also asked me, "How's your mother's weight? She's been known to fluctuate."

When I got back to New York, I repeated that story to my mother. She went ballistic: "That son of a bitch. How dare he!" she shouted. "I was always small when I was with him." It was like they were eighteen again and cussing each other out. He knew it was the perfect dig to get at my mother, and he knew that I would tell her about it. We both played our parts, just as he figured we would.

After the gun range, we went back to the house. My step-mother was in another room, and my father and I were standing in the small hallway between the kitchen and the living room. We were watching his daughter play on the thick sandy-brown carpet in front of the fireplace. She was just a happy, beautiful blond toddler keeping herself entertained. The house was decorated for the holidays, and it was very homey.

"So, how did you end up with Fallon?" I asked my father, trying to make small talk.

"Well," he said, "Bridget never had any children before, and I never had any children, so, you know."

He quickly caught himself, realizing he'd made a massive mistake. The air became heavy, and it was incredibly silent between us. We really looked into each other's eyes and processed everything that was packed into his statement. It rolled over me all at once in a wave that made my arm hair stand on end. In his mind, I had never even existed. He had erased me.

I stood there in silence. I shouldn't have been so surprised, since everything in his life announced this truth—he had never reached out, and the people at the station didn't know about me.

"Oh, I'm so sorry," he said. He gave me a hug and said, "I have you now, and I'm not going to let you go."

Even as he said those words, I knew the score. I knew that there was nothing here for me. Whatever I was searching for by getting to know him, it wasn't there to be found. There would be no fairy-tale ending.

On my father's part, that statement was an innocent mistake. And it was the innocence of his mistake that confirmed that we didn't need to have a relationship. It wasn't that he thought poorly of me. He didn't think about me at all.

We got through the rest of the weekend. My father and stepmother were perfect hosts. They were trying really hard, but I knew that this experiment in a new relationship was doomed.

When I got back to New York and told Renee about what happened, she got a little angry and said, "I'm sorry." She gave me a hug. It felt like a favorite blanket. "I'm not surprised something like that happened," she said. She knew much more of my father's history than I did. She was more disappointed by the news than I ever would be.

Nicolas called a few times after that, but our communication petered out. Neither of us tried very hard to pursue it. To this day, my son, Thomas, has never met him. Even though they have so much in common—my son's a police officer in California, just like my father was—they probably never will meet.

The day I turned forty, I remember turning to my husband,

Tom, and saying, "Do you think my father thinks of me on special days like today?"

"There is no good in even asking that question," Tom said. That was absolutely the right answer. It wasn't yes or no. It was, "That kind of thinking isn't going to make your life better."

I don't hate men. I don't blame men for the way I was treated by my father. I don't think that I have an older husband now because I needed a dad, even if that's a temptingly easy suggestion. I love having someone who really knows his shit and has an incredible brain. Tom's age alone doesn't account for those qualities. Many of the men I've been in relationships with have been much closer to my age. My first husband was older than me, but only by seven years. The fact that Tom is thirty-three years older is not my blueprint—it's just how things happened to shake out the one time everything else clicked.

I don't think the father figures who let me down are bad people. They were doing the best they could, and sometimes that's just not enough. It's less their fault than it is the circumstances they were in. I can't really blame them for what happened.

Now I'm so far away from these issues that it doesn't hurt anymore. In those moments, it was excruciating, but you can't stay in that pain too long. You have to let it wash over you and pass, or else it will drown you. I also have to be mindful that these rejections don't make me hard-hearted. It can be difficult to trust other people. I'm always waiting for the other shoe to drop, like someone could walk out of my life at a moment's notice. But I have to evolve beyond that mind-set.

I have to transcend those people and the pain they brought me. I have to keep walking forward. I have to do the best that I can and hope that everything I've learned from these men helps me do things better than they did.

4

SO HOT IT BURNS

*W*hen Tom and I fly our Gulfstream to New York City, we land at Teterboro Airport. It's just across the Hudson River from Manhattan in Bergen County, New Jersey. Like most airports, it's not necessarily in the most glamorous part of town. If Manhattan is the city that never sleeps, this is the stretch of New Jersey that passes out in the gutter. As our car pulls out of Teterboro toward Manhattan, we turn down a service road that looks like it has definitely seen a body or two disposed of in the past. On that road, right across the street from the airport, is a square, white, run-down building sitting in the corner of a parking lot. This is Shakers, one of New Jersey's infamous go-go bars.

In New Jersey, clubs that feature nudity can't also serve

alcohol. To get around this law, there are many go-go clubs and bikini bars. Girls dance wearing as little as they can, while still keeping it legal for guys to unwind with a beer after work. There are several of them near Teterboro, but Shakers loomed large because of its visibility right across the street. I felt unsettled every time Tom and I drove past it, because it was like a ghost from the past. Once upon a time, a whole lifetime ago, I was one of those girls shaking it at Shakers.

Tom knew vaguely about this particular bullet point on my résumé, but we'd never discussed it in detail. I certainly never told him about any of the clubs I worked in or what it was like. It's not a time in my life that I'm fond of recalling.

After I graduated from Northside High in Atlanta, my mother and I both moved to New York City on October 1, 1989. I knew I needed to be in the big city where there were more opportunities to get my start as an entertainer. For Renee, it was the perfect excuse to leave her old life and disappointments behind. She quit her job in the mortgage industry and got another job in Manhattan doing the same thing at a different bank. Renee was always an artist, working on paintings and teaching the piano. She wanted more for her life than just raising a kid in Atlanta. She would say, "Erika needs to leave, and I need to be there because she can't do anything by herself." What she really meant was that she wanted to leave just as badly as I did.

We were living at 215 West 84th Street and Broadway on the Upper West Side. It's a nice doorman building where Edgar Allan Poe used to have a farmhouse, so it was a pretty cool spot. We lived in a spacious one-bedroom apartment that had a loft over the kitchen. Renee got the bedroom and I slept in the loft. For those unfamiliar with the quirks of New York City apartments, there was a little ladder in the living room that went up to a platform that was over the kitchen, but the open part of the loft looked out onto the living room. You couldn't stand up in it, but it was big enough for a bed and my artwork on the walls. There were no fights over closet space, because I barely owned anything—just a leather jacket, a few pairs of jeans, and dancewear. I wasn't a fashionista back then. I was broke.

I had no connections in New York, but I did have a couple of high school friends who also moved up there to pursue their dreams. We were all eighteen to twenty, and we didn't know shit. Just like every other theater kid, I was trying to live out some would-be dream of being in show business. I just wanted to perform. I wanted to get a job doing what I was trained to do: singing, dancing, and acting. It's like that line from "The Music and the Mirror" in *A Chorus Line*, "Give me somebody to dance for, give me somebody to show. Let me wake up in the morning to find I have somewhere exciting to go."

While I was taking the subway all over town going to auditions, I still needed to make some cash. My mom was thirty-six and trying to start fresh. She told me, "You're eighteen. Pay rent or get out." And she meant it. Our rent was not cheap, especially for an eighteen-year-old with more promise than income.

My girlfriend Justine had graduated from Northside before me and immediately moved to New York. When I got to town, she became my best friend and we were inseparable—hanging out, preparing for auditions, and going to all the clubs we could charm our way into. We were both broke, but Justine had it even harder than I did. At least I had my mother in case things got really bad. Justine only had herself. I've always admired her, because she went through a lot on her own. I don't know if I could have done the same without Renee.

This was 1989, before Mayor Giuliani showed up with his magic wand and Disney-fied large swaths of New York. Justine's apartment was on the far Upper West Side, and the stroller set was still a good decade from showing up and transforming the place.

Justine's apartment had recently been renovated, so it was nice inside. When I would spend the night, I would sleep on what we called the San Francisco futon, because it had lumps as big as hills. But the neighborhood was trouble, and she got robbed a lot. It looked a bit like that movie *New Jack City* where there were just empty lots all around and some of the buildings were condemned. You could hear gunshots daily. It was that rough.

We were both incredibly broke, riding the subway to all of our auditions and subsisting on grilled cheese sandwiches and dollar slices of pizza when we could afford them. One day Justine said, "Erika, I have a dancing job for us."

I was like, "Okay, what is it?"

"It's kind of like the movie *Flashdance*. You can perform and you wear something that resembles a swimsuit. It's like a cross between that and a nightclub," she said. "And it's in New Jersey, right outside the Holland Tunnel."

"What are you talking about?" I asked. It seemed too crazy to be true and, well, not exactly how I was looking to start my career as an entertainer. But *Flashdance* was one of my favorite movies.

"Just come with me. It's going to be fine and we'll make some cash," she said.

One Friday night, we took the subway from her apartment down to the Port Authority and then rode the bus out to New Jersey. This in itself was a treacherous journey. I remember avoiding the rats on the subway platform, and every time I got out of the Port Authority with my life I said a little prayer of thanks.

The first club I worked in was called the Palace, in Passaic, New Jersey. It was located in a narrow limestone building like you might find on an old-fashioned New England Main Street. There was a small window in the facade with a busted mannequin wearing hideous lingerie. It was creepy and sad. This was not the glamorous life that I had imagined for myself. I thought, *This is so gross. Why am I here?*

Looking back on it, I think Justine just wanted someone to tag along with her because she hated it so much. Sometimes you had to go by yourself, and it was depressing as hell. At least if there are two of you, there's someone to complain to and it's not as scary and lonely.

When I arrived I met Gino, the guy who owned the club. He was wearing a cream-colored cashmere overcoat and had a gray John Gotti–style blowout. He wore a pinky ring, drove a white Mercedes, and always seemed to be taking cash out of the register. He could have been a character in *Goodfellas*.

Justine took me up to the dressing room and gave me one of her outfits to wear. It was a cobalt-blue Brazilian bikini. That was the hot thing in these clubs back then, basically the smallest bikini you could imagine, with tiny ties on the side and little triangles of fabric for the top.

When we got there, Justine told me to call her Justice. She felt like it had a little bit more exotic flair than Justine. She was trying to create a more glamorous stage persona. I just went by Erika.

At the Palace, like at most of the bars, the girls would dance for thirty minutes and then have thirty minutes off. As we waited upstairs, the DJ would try to get people to stay by announcing over the broken, crackling PA which girls should get ready. If they knew that fresh faces (and fresh everything else) would be out soon, maybe they'd stick around for another drink. The DJ would say, "Erika, five minutes. Veronica, five minutes. Robin, five minutes." To this day, I still laugh thinking about it.

Most of the bars were set up the same way—a square bar in the middle of the room with a square stage in the center of the bar. As we were dancing on the stage in our bikinis, a well where the bartenders stood, plus the bar itself, kept the patrons off of us.

Though many might want to call it one, this wasn't a strip club. There were no lap dances or glamorous champagne rooms or anything like that. This was just dancing in a microbikini and talking to the guys—all blue-collar dudes after work—for their extra singles. At the end of the night, we'd have to cash in those dollar bills with the bartender to take home larger bills.

The first time I did it I felt fucking insane. I was wearing this blue bikini, which seemed like it should feel familiar. It was just slightly smaller than the leotards and dance costumes I'd been performing in for most of my life. But I knew that my goal here was to hustle money, and that made it feel scandalous.

This wasn't even as fabulous as being a stripper for real. I was just dipping my foot in the baby pool. There are girls at eighteen, living in Vegas, and working at the Spearmint Rhino, making boatloads of cash. I wish it had been something exciting like that, but none of that was happening in suburban New Jersey. The other girls and I weren't that caliber of talent. We weren't the women who allegedly make five to ten grand a night at some upscale strip club. It just wasn't that place, didn't have that clientele, and couldn't draw that level of talent, because there wasn't the audience for them.

Don't get me wrong—I looked cute. I weighed 118 pounds and had a lean dancer's body. This was way before my boob job, so I was small and natural. I looked like this little tomboy running around in a bikini. It was a marketable look, to say the least.

That first night when I got on stage, Justine told me to just watch her and figure it out. I didn't know if I was supposed to do choreography or what. I had no clue what I was doing, but she'd let me know if I was missing signals for guys to tip me or if I was hanging out in the well of the bar too long, which Gino didn't like. I had no clue. I was just trying to pay the rent so I could go out and audition one more time. When the club closed at 3 a.m., I had a few hundred dollars more in my backpack than when we started. Considering this was the eighties in Jersey, it wasn't bad for a first night.

The Palace had that gross bar smell of cigarettes and stale beer. It was set up like a saloon, a long room with very high ceilings. For some reason there were multicolored streamers and half-inflated balloons along the ceiling, like a perpetual New Year's Eve party gone wrong. We would stink when we left, because back then customers were still allowed to smoke indoors. The stench would get in our hair. The lighting wasn't particularly flattering, either, with blue and pink lights hitting us from above. They tried to make the atmosphere sexy and have us look our best, but when you're in a club that smells of cooking grease and day-old Newports, there's not that much you can do about the mood.

As far as the dancing itself goes, I was pretty good, once I figured it out. When you take as many dance classes as I did growing up, you learn how to control your body. Not necessarily in a sexual way, but it is feminine. Combine that with knowing how to captivate an audience and keep it engaged, which I learned from performing, and I figured I had a pretty good recipe for getting these guys' attention.

I would always have to beg the DJ to play dance music or house music—anything with a beat that I could actually dance to. Otherwise it would be lots of New Jersey hairband rock: Bon Jovi, Def Leppard, Poison, Whitesnake. That stuff is impossible to dance to. All you can do is whip your hair around and pretend you're in the "Hot for Teacher" video.

I started doing these clubs two nights a week, on Fridays and Saturdays, because that was all I could handle. Those were the good nights when you could make the most money. There was a little circuit of all of these clubs, and I would find out from the other girls which ones were hot, where you could make money, which ones were slowing down, and where the action was. It was then up to me to make connections at those clubs and try to get booked there.

I went all over, from Secaucus to Newark and everywhere in between. These clubs all had names like Shakers, Bunns, the Palace, AJ's, or The Navel Base. The Navel Base was actually seized by the Feds at some point when I was making the rounds, and no one ever went there again. I danced once at Satin Dolls in Lodi, New Jersey, which is where they shot the scenes in *The Sopranos* set at Bada Bing! Shakers burned down at one point.

After they rebuilt it, they sold shirts that said, Shakers: So Hot It Burns. Yeah, it was *that* cheesy.

Some of the girls who worked in the club had a side business where they would make tiny outfits and the Brazilian bikinis. One girl had a company called Itsy Bitsy, and I bought a bunch of different outfits from her. At the end of a shift I'd fork over a hundred dollars of the money I just made and walk out with new outfits: a fluorescent orange one, a royal blue one, and a sheer black one that made me look like Apollonia or one of those other Prince girls from the eighties.

The aesthetic was very much big hair, deep tans, denim jackets, and all of those clichés you can think of. Basically everyone looked a little like Snooki, even though she hadn't been born yet, and was hosed down in sickly sweet candy-apple-scented body spray. I thought of a strategy to make myself stand out, which is how I would make all of my tips. I had long, straight blond hair all the way down my back. I kept my alabaster skin natural, and I would wear bright red lipstick. While all the other girls wore pumps or stilettos, I would wear sexy ankle boots with high heels. Today I perform in over-the-knee boots, so it's still basically the same idea.

One of the biggest lessons I learned was that not every man likes the same thing, and this fact applied to me. Blondes with a southern twang don't always win. I would walk up to a guy thinking that he was going to give me the cash, but no. He only liked redheads or he only liked black girls or he only wanted someone with a fuller body. You never knew what they were going to want just by looking at them.

Most of the customers were really nice people, but not the kind who were going to help my career. I remember this one guy who would always be at the club. He had a Jheri curl glistening under his captain's hat, and he would flip his dentures around in his mouth. I'd be dancing onstage and hear this weird squishy, clicking noise. I'd look over and his teeth were upside down in his mouth. That said, he was a very nice man and a great tipper.

There were plenty of times when I had guys who would pinch or pull at me while I was working. The guys could smell how naive I was and they were always trying to get close or asking me to go out on dates. I always said no. I never saw any illegal activity going on, but looking back, it might have been all around me. I was just too young and stupid to know what to look for.

Other than the clientele, one of the worst parts of working at the club was the transportation issue. Getting there on the bus was a drag, but even worse was getting home. The buses would stop running at a certain hour, and neither of us wanted to drop half of the money we made to take a cab home. It was cold as hell in the winter, and you didn't want to be hanging around outside waiting for your ride in these sketchy New Jersey neighborhoods. You would end up a statistic.

This was way before Uber, but one of the ways we would get home was this guy we called Lobotomy John. He was a freelance driver who would pick up all the girls from the clubs and drive them into the city. All the girls lived in Manhattan, trying to make it as actresses, models, or dancers, and they had to work the clubs to pay for these expensive apartments. He wasn't dangerous or anything, he was just slightly . . . off. He had a route and would drive around to all the clubs and pick up the girls, packing four or five of them into the backseat of his Cadillac. This was usually where we would "network" to find out which were the good clubs for making money.

Every time he'd come into the club he'd say, "I'm going to the diner. Do you want me to bring you something?" We would say no as politely as possible. Then he'd say, "You're sure you don't want a fruit cup?" Every time it was a fruit cup. No matter what you answered, he would say, "Do you want a fruit cup?"

"No, I don't want a fruit cup!" I would say in exasperation. He was just being sweet and asking if he could get us anything, but every time it was, "Do you want a fruit cup? Do you want a fruit cup?" One day, just to see what all the fuss was about, I let him get me a fruit cup. You know what? It was amazing! Just kidding . . . it wasn't that great.

With or without Lobotomy John, getting home was always a pain in the ass. One night Justine came up to me and said, "Hey, some friends of mine are going to take us home." These friends were a band that Justine knew from the city that coincidentally wound up at the club. She was so embarrassed!

I got dressed in the dressing room and came out wearing my typical black sweatshirt, jeans, boots, and backpack. The night was over and my hair was in a ponytail, but I still had on my bright red lipstick.

I met Justine in the parking lot and she said, "Oh, there they are." Up pulled this van and the door opened. The back of the van had wall-to-wall carpet and captain's chairs and shit. It looked like Bon Jovi was in there. They were like, "Yo, come on, man. Get on in."

I was skeptical. "Are these your friends?" I asked Justine.

She said, "Yeah, they're cool. They have a gig in the city. They're going to drop us off on the way."

I was thinking that I'd rather be eating a fruit cup with Lobotomy John than dealing with this scene. There was just something sketchy about this whole plan.

They were playing music and the vibe was just bizarre. Then the driver said, "We've got to stop by my house. I'm just going to run in and get something."

We stopped at a house in a typical suburban New Jersey

neighborhood, where the houses are all two stories tall, with aluminum siding and dead lawns, and crammed next to each other like passengers on a commuter train. Someone's girlfriend was out on the street with her friend. The driver slid back the door so his bandmates could get out, and she saw Justine and me sitting there. She screamed, "Oh my God. I knew it. I knew it! I knew you were hanging out with strippers."

A fight broke out with the girlfriend and the driver right there in the middle of the street at 3 a.m. I was surprised the neighbors didn't call the cops, or at least shout out the window for them to shut up.

"Justine, all of this so we could save twenty-five dollars?" I asked her.

The whole band got into a fight with this girlfriend and her friend. She shouted, "I knew you were in there with a couple of whores." She pronounced it in that New Jersey accent that sounds like "whoo-wahs." They brushed her aside and drove off with us in the back. They were very sweet, but I didn't need all of this.

I wanted to tell that girl, "Bitch, I am not a whore. I am just trying to get back to the city. I don't even want to be doing this job. I hate this entire existence. I don't know these fucking people. I just want a ride home." But I didn't do any of that. I just sat in the back of this carpeted van, hugging my knees and waiting for the fight to be over so I could get home and pass the fuck out.

Another night I was working at one of the clubs and Anthony, the manager, called me up to the office. He was sexy, only had one eye, and rocked the hell out of an eye patch. Once the door was closed, he said to me, "Erika, what are you doing?"

I thought I was doing a good job dancing at the club. I said to him, "What do you mean, what am I doing?"

"What are you doing here?" he asked.

"I'm just trying to make some money to pay my rent. Why?"

"Where's your father?" he asked.

I told him that I didn't know my father and we didn't have a relationship.

"You don't belong here," Anthony told me finally.

At the time, I was offended and confused. But really, Anthony was my gangster angel. He knew I had more to offer than just dancing in his club. He knew I had something else to give, and I wasn't cut out for this lifestyle.

I was pretty awful at this gig. I was insulted if the guys didn't give me money. I thought, *Come on, dude. I'm smiling. It's not a lot of money. Give it up.* I never wanted to be there, so I never really put my back into it, so to speak.

I got fired from a couple of places because I was such an

asshole. At the Palace, you had to call to confirm that you were going to work your assigned shifts. I thought that was stupid, so I wouldn't confirm. My word was my word, so if I said I was going to be there on Friday, I would be there on Friday. After warning me a few times, and me getting sassy with them, they stopped booking me entirely. Can you imagine getting fired from a fucking go-go bar in New Jersey? Do you know how lazy and ill-tempered you have to be to get fired from a gig like that?

One night at Go-Go-Rama—one of the clubs that would hire as many dancers as they could squish onto the stage—I looked over at Justine and said to her onstage, screaming over some obnoxious music, "This is a dumb concept. We have on stupid bikinis, writhing around, trying to get cash for the rent. This is dumb." And it was hard because there were so many girls it was impossible to make any money. Don't get me wrong, my floor work is second to none. If you don't believe me, watch my "Painkillr" video on YouTube. A lot of the moves I use as Erika Jayne I perfected in New Jersey. Still, as a concept, I thought it was dumb.

Go-go dancing wasn't the only moneymaker then, but it was a dependable source of income in a pinch. You knew you were going to make some money at the end of the night, and that was something.

I wish I had some big, dramatic story about how this stage

of my life ended. How one night I was finally fired by some wannabe Mafia boss who was sick of my rebellious ass. Or I was just so tired of the Port Authority, the customers flipping their dentures, Lobotomy John shilling for fruit cups, and all the other bullshit we had to go through, that I walked out in a blaze of glory and never looked back. But honestly, it wasn't that dramatic. I got a job cocktail waitressing at a little bar in the West Village. It was a lot easier to get to, and I made about the same amount of money while retaining much more dignity. This was also about the same time I started dating the man who would become my first husband and my son's father, so I didn't really want to be shaking it at Shakers anymore.

The reason I don't like looking back on this period has nothing to do with taking my clothes off or nudity or anything like that. I still take my clothes off today, and I have no problem with it. It's not a moral judgment. I just wasn't prepared for the scene, and I was totally outmatched. I remember thinking this was how people got stuck. There was always an aura of sadness that I didn't like. There was a resignation, and I wasn't going to let it infect me.

I never had much occasion to think about that time in my life until Tom and I started flying into Teterboro. Right across the street was Shakers, every time. Each trip to New York, I knew there was going to be that little bit of dread. We would drive by it, and I would have to decide whether or not I was going to tell Tom my story.

Finally, one day as we were driving past, I decided it was time to come clean. I knew Tom loved me. This wouldn't make him think any less of the woman I had become in the decade since I finally walked out of that club. As we drove by, I said, "Hey, Tom. See that place over there?"

Immediately, he knew what was up. "Is that one of the clubs where you worked?" he asked.

"Yup," I replied somewhat bashfully.

"Well, we have to go. Come on, let's check it out." We told the driver to turn around, and we headed for the club.

Now this was a Tuesday afternoon or something like that. Not really prime time for a New Jersey go-go bar. When we walked through those front doors, I felt like I was walking into the past. Everything was the same: the square bar, the lighting overhead, the blue-collar guys drinking beer out of the same green and brown bottles. There was even the same smell, which is what really brought me back.

Tom and I sat down and got drinks. We watched the one lonely day-shift girl halfheartedly work the stage. She wore all white, and it glowed under the black light. The lighting also made her blond hair glow bright yellow. She looked just like I must have when I was there. She was doing her job, but I'm sure wishing she was somewhere else. Tom asked me about how the clubs work and what I remembered about my time there. I told him the whole story. We didn't stay that long and honestly, I was happy to leave.

We got back into the car and headed off toward Manhattan. Tom reached over, grabbed my hand, and looked me right in the eyes. "Look, Erika," he said. "On the bright side, it only took you ten years to get across the street." We both burst out laughing.

He was right, and I think I'm a better person for it. I've never been one to knock where someone else comes from or what they had to do to get where they are today. It's easy for people to pass judgment. I never like slut shaming or any other kind of shaming. I always want to tell people that when you're putting a dollar in a woman's bra, you have no idea whom you're tipping. You don't know what is going to happen to anyone or where they'll end up. I certainly never look down on a woman hustling to make a buck. I've been that woman, and all of that hustling makes every buck even more precious.

I learned the value of a dollar at Shakers. Sitting in the Gulfstream across the street a decade later, I still knew it. That is the real lesson of money. You earn your self-worth working for those stupid dollars. I always dreamed so big that I could imagine one day having my own airplane, even though I didn't understand there was a private airport across the street from the very spot I was scrounging for tips. That old part of me is always going to be there. Shakers is always going to be greeting me every time I land at Teterboro. It's an old ghost, reaching out from the murky past. "Remember me?" it asks.

I always acknowledge, "Yes. Yes, I do."

5

A PLAYDATE WITH EVERY BOY

*W*hen I was in kindergarten, I had a playdate with every boy in my class. My mother used to keep my pink Huffy Thunder Rose bike in the trunk of her car, because I was always off to some boy's house after school. We would ride bikes, catch turtles, climb trees, and play in the mud. I was a bit of a tomboy, so it made sense to hang out with the boys in my class rather than the girls. But also, let's just say I have always enjoyed the company of the opposite sex.

My mom says that I was flirty even as a toddler. I was really social, very open, and showered people with affection. I was always putting on the ritz, picking out short shorts and crop tops that would fashionably express my carefree attitude.

In second grade, I kissed my first boy. It was just a peck on the lips. The class was watching a movie, and one of the boys in the class and I snuck a kiss while sitting under the desks. I never thought of myself as pretty as a child. There was always someone prettier, blonder, or taller in my class. I didn't think that my looks set me apart. What I did have was a comfort level with myself, which people found infectious.

My first serious boyfriend was Jonathan, in high school. He was in the Tech Department at Northside High School and I was in the Musical Theater Department. Jonathan was not only hot but also incredibly bright and always made honor roll. He had deep blue eyes and was a junior, whereas I was only a freshman. I think I caught his eye on one of those Northside spring break trips to Europe and we got together at the end of that year. He was fun and a little wild, but a really great guy and treated me well. Both my grandmother and mother loved him.

I lost my virginity to him when I was fourteen. We were in his bedroom at his parents' house and the Eagles' "Hotel California" was playing on the stereo. Was that a little foreshadowing of my West Coast life to come? He wasn't a virgin, but he wanted to be a gentleman and not push me. I was ready and I had to convince him of that. Jonathan is still a great guy, and we are in touch to this day.

While Jonathan was handsome, I don't really have a physical type. I'm too enamored with male energy to really care if a guy is short or tall, blond or brunette, hairy or smooth. I've always loved men. I love the way they smell, I love the way they taste, I love the way they feel. So, physically, my relationships have been all over the map. I had some really gorgeous boyfriends and some really nerdy boyfriends.

What I am most attracted to are intelligent, aggressive, successful men. Beautiful men are great, and God bless them, but that's not who I would choose as a partner. Another similarity among the men I choose is that both of my husbands are Italian. I always like to joke that I marry Italians, date Jewish guys, and as for the rest—I'm going to keep that to myself.

There's only one time I had a same-sex encounter. To be fair, it was more of a three-way situation. An ex-boyfriend I kept in touch with had married an acquaintance of mine. He was about six feet tall, muscular, educated, and professional. She was a light-skinned Caribbean beauty with golden highlights in her dark hair. They were a handsome couple. He called me and asked me to go out to dinner with them on Valentine's Day.

We had a great time, kind of like we were on a little date. They seemed like they were testing the waters with me and driving the conversation toward sex. He had already hinted they were into this kind of thing, so I wasn't totally shocked. I knew this might be on the agenda, and I was okay with it. We went back to their place after dinner and had quite the memorable Valentine's Day.

It was a very positive experience, I had a great time with the two of them, and it satisfied my curiosity.

Among all of my friends, I have the most boring sex stories. But in my defense, I hang around with a bunch of libertines. I've almost always been more of a relationship type. I got married and had a child at twenty. Then I married again at twenty-seven. Even between marriages I almost always had a boyfriend, so I wasn't really playing the field. I enjoy having a partner. I enjoy companionship, having a best friend—all of that wrapped up into one.

I met my first husband, Tom (but we'll call him Tommy to avoid any confusion with my current husband), during one of the rare single periods of my life. I moved to New York when I was eighteen. I was going to auditions, working, and going out to clubs in Manhattan. My high school girlfriend Justine and I went out like it was our job. There was one month where we didn't see the sunlight at all. We'd wake up late, audition, and then go out to the club. As the sun was coming up, we would go pass out at her place.

Like a good New Yorker, I was always dressed in black: black jeans, black top, black leather jacket. It was the late eighties and early nineties, so we were at Palladium, Larry Tee's Love Machine, Red Zone, Twilo, MK, The World, Sound Factory, and all the legendary superclubs. It was the era of the club kids and one of the best times of my life. I was doing all of the hedonistic partying that most kids get out of their systems in college.

One of our favorites was the China Club, which had a legendary Monday night party. Back then, it was in the basement of the Beacon Hotel on 73rd Street on the Upper West Side. It became known as a cool hangout for musicians who might spontaneously stop by and play. We're talking people like Stevie Nicks, David Bowie, and Stevie Wonder. Madonna even had Thanksgiving dinner there one year.

Monday night was their biggest night, and you wouldn't even get through the door if you weren't cool enough. This was the era of the door policy in New York, way before bottle service took over. Now, anyone can pay their way to get into a nightclub. Back then, if you didn't look right, you wouldn't get past the bouncer.

The great thing about the China Club was the crowd was always the perfect mix. It was black and white, gay and straight, rich and poor; it was just the coolest of the cool. You'd have the downtown stockbrokers mixing with the sexy uptown Domini-cans who always had the best blow, which they called "fish scale."

We saw Mike Tyson, Rick James, Michael Jordan, Guns N' Roses, and Eddie Murphy all hanging out at the China Club. Justine texted me recently and reminded me of the time we were at the China Club and she could have gone home with a certain rapper turned underwear model, but didn't. She's still mad at herself for not pursuing it. I am, too!

I wasn't going after any celebs, though. I was after the DJ. He was a tall, muscular Sicilian with the kind of streetwise swagger that only native New Yorkers can muster. He was an absolute piece. I pointed him out to Justine and said, "He's so sexy to me."

"Well, you know him," Justine said.

"Um, I don't think so," I said.

"No, you know him," she said. "I swear."

To this day, I think that Justine was absolutely nuts. At the time, he had recently broken up with the famous Penthouse Pet named Sandi Korn. (She later dated Donald Trump, and he convinced her to change her name to Sandra Taylor.) I noticed him way before he noticed me. He had no reason to. I was some skinny, loudmouthed kid from the South. He had just gotten out of a relationship with a girl whose poster was on the wall of every horny teenager jerking off in America.

I don't remember exactly how, but after seeing him around the club for a while, I eventually ended up with his phone number on a little slip of paper. We had something in common, because I was performing and making music, and he was playing music at the club. That was the start of the conversation right there.

I was nineteen and he was twenty-six. Tommy was raised right, and he really knew how to treat a woman. His father died when he was young. His mother was in the garment industry, so he helped her with the family business. DJing was just a side gig he started as a teenager in clubs around town, but he kept doing it mostly because he enjoyed it. Like all of my boyfriends, he was very smart. He even skipped a grade because he was so bright.

While dating, we were doing all of those classic New York activities: going to the theater and museums, walking in Central Park, and having dinner in the nicest places. Of course, we were also going out to the clubs a lot. I kept visiting the China Club every Monday so I could hang out with him.

One night he was DJing and some record executives were in the crowd, as well as a few of Tommy's old DJ friends. He came out and said hi to all of us, then he said, "You know what? I'm going to get in the booth and play all old disco shit, just because." He had all of his old records on him from the seventies. He just started playing all the classics that he grew up loving. Everyone in the club fucking lost their minds, and we danced even harder and longer that night than we usually did.

After about six months of dating, I moved in with Tommy. I wanted to take the relationship to the next level, but I was also ready to move out of the loft space over Renee's kitchen.

I moved into his apartment in a brick building on the Upper West Side, at 100th Street and Amsterdam. The apartment was a recently renovated one-bedroom, with a loft over the kitchen—just like the one I was moving out of.

While we were living there, I missed a few days of my birth control pills. I thought I could double up on the next ones and it would work out fine. Well, it didn't. My period was late. It dawned on me in an acting class while we were doing some exercises. Somebody was performing a boring scene, and for the first time I wondered if I was pregnant. I didn't feel pregnant, but then again, I had no idea what being pregnant felt like.

That afternoon, I went home and took a home pregnancy test. It was positive. A few days later, I went to my OB/GYN,

Dr. Cox (a great gynecologist with the world's most ironic name). She confirmed that I was pregnant.

I was just kind of fascinated by the news, because it didn't even seem like a possibility to me. It was never part of my plan. I'd never really even held a baby before. Being a mother wasn't something that I was thinking about, even in the abstract. But from the moment I found out, I knew that I was going to keep my baby. In a weird way, I knew that he needed to be born.

When Tommy got home, I told him the news. He was as surprised as I was, but he was very sweet about it. We decided then and there that we were going to get married, start a family, and do right by our child.

My mother wasn't nearly as thrilled. Renee had gotten pregnant with me at a young age, and that derailed a lot of her dreams. I think she was upset when she saw the same thing happening to me.

Renee said, "This isn't going to work out well. Your life will be changed forever, and I don't think this is the responsible thing for you to do. You should have thought better." She said that once I had a baby, people would look at me like "a used car." My grandmother wasn't thrilled, either. No one was trying to talk me out of having my son, but they were all giving me their bitter truth—that I had a very difficult road ahead of me.

Tommy and I got married at St. Patrick's Cathedral in Manhattan in December 1991. The wedding was big, obnoxious, and pink. My bridesmaids—who included Trish and Tracy from the girl group The Flirts, with whom I had recorded—wore puffy pink gowns. They were the same color as a Sweet'N Low packet. They looked like cupcakes as they walked down the aisle.

In hindsight, those dresses were hideous, but mine was gorgeous. At the time, I was doing some modeling for a company called Timeless Bridal. When the bridal boutique buyers came looking for gowns, I would model the products. From them, I bought an incredibly elegant ivory silk gown sprinkled with tiny pink rosettes. It was really classic and had great movement. My grandfather Hollis walked me down the aisle. I even had a beautiful veil with ivory satin trim and a row of matching rosettes across the top.

The location was perfect. I'll never forget the sight as I walked from the altar to the doors of St. Patrick's Cathedral on Fifth Avenue, along with having our wedding photos taken in front of the giant Christmas tree in Rockefeller Plaza.

We moved apartments again, this time down to Battery Park City, at the tip of Manhattan. Tommy's mother lived down there, and with the baby on the way it made sense. It was a brand-new development, so that was where everyone was

moving to start families in Manhattan. It was a doorman building at 280 Rector Place, and we were the first people to live in
our apartment. It was a one-bedroom—without a loft, finally.
When the baby came, he slept in a crib in our bedroom.

When I got pregnant, I weighed 118 pounds (about twenty
pounds less than I weigh now). For the first time in my life, I
started to cook all my own food. I was going to the grocery
store every day and making my own pasta, preparing my own
salads, and cooking my own meat. I was very disciplined and
keeping my diet very healthy for the baby and me. Then, on
Friday at noon I would allow myself my one small indulgence:
a can of Coke and a Snickers bar.

When I delivered my son, I was only 128 pounds. When
I was pregnant on the subway, no one ever got up and gave
me their seat because I didn't look pregnant at all. People were
worried that I didn't gain enough weight, but then I delivered a
perfectly healthy six-pound, eight-ounce baby. I would like to
take this opportunity to thank my son for not giving me stretch
marks on my tummy.

My pregnancy was easy, but I did have terrible morning
sickness. Once it got so bad that I had to get off the subway
and run to one of the garbage cans on the platform at the
72nd Street station. I barfed out what seemed like just about
everything I had ever possibly eaten. I must have been hugging

that disgusting can for about fifteen minutes. Several women walked by and asked me if I was okay. Only someone who had gone through pregnancy would know exactly what that struggle was like.

Seven months after my wedding, I was about two weeks from my due date. I woke up with a terrible backache. I called my mother and she said, "Erika, you have to call the doctor. That is early labor."

I called Dr. Cox and she said, "It sounds like it's happening. You better come into the hospital so we can check it out." I had what is called "back labor." The ache was from my son's head pressing on the small of my back. I told Tommy to go get a cab to take us from our apartment downtown all the way up to New York Hospital on the Upper East Side.

"But in Lamaze class they said that you should walk around," he told me.

"Just get me a cab!" I said, freaking out a little.

"No. We're broke and you need to walk around," he insisted. We walked to the 6 train station at Wall Street and took that for what seemed like an eternity to the hospital. No one got up and gave me their seat even then. I was in labor on fucking public transportation.

I gave birth to my son at 6 p.m., and it was an easy delivery.

He was not crying when he came out. He was just kind of looking around, with his big blue eyes, which were sensitive to the light. He was turning his head back and forth as if he was thinking, *Where the fuck am I?* Finally, they smacked him on his pink behind and he started crying.

When the doctor put him into my arms, it wasn't like I was meeting a stranger for the first time. I felt like we were two souls being reunited after a long break. Like meeting an old friend. *Oh, hey. There you are,* I thought as I held him in the hospital. *Welcome back.* We named him Thomas, after his father.

After he was born, the first phone call I made was to my grandmother to tell her the news. Renee was just across town, but I didn't call her. Twenty-five years later, I think that still bothers my mother. Maybe she shouldn't have called me a used car? Maybe then she would have gotten the first call.

As I mentioned, I had never really held a baby before. But instinctually, I knew how to do everything. My mother and grandmother were shocked at how quickly I learned to hold him, swaddle him, feed him, and figure out just what he needed. I loved having the little one. He was so portable. I could just wrap him up and take him out. It helped that my son was a very easy baby. He was never colicky, never fussed much, and was sleeping through the night pretty early.

Everything else about life as a young mother wasn't very exciting, though. I had to put my career goals to the side while I was taking care of the baby. Most of my friends from before were still young and more interested in going out than in taking my baby to the park.

When we moved to Battery Park City, I was pretty isolated. There was nothing down there except one Gristedes grocery store and it wasn't even that good. Some of the sidewalks weren't paved yet, because they were still constructing buildings down there. There was just dirt with a rope next to the open space. I would be walking around with the baby completely by myself. We could go down to the water, but in the fall and winter that wind would tear through us, making me miserable, and upsetting the baby.

Like a sugar cube on your tongue, the girl group I was working with, The Flirts, had dissolved. My bridesmaid and friend Tracy was finally using her economics degree to work with her father trading semiprecious metals down in the Financial District, which was not far from our house. I would walk over to her office—the same office that John D. Rockefeller had—and we would go out to lunch. But if the market got hot, I'd have to sit there and wait for her to finish trading, which could take forever.

Other than that, I didn't have any friends in the neighborhood. Sometimes when we would go to the park, other women would ask me, "Oh, who do you work for?" Assuming that because I was so young, I had to be this kid's nanny. I would point to Thomas and answer, "This guy."

I would take him out almost every day. Often we'd walk over to the World Trade Center, because there was an indoor mall and we could walk around without being stuck in the weather. I can still visualize every step, feature, storefront, and doorman on the walk from our apartment to the World Trade Center.

One February day it was snowing. I decided not to go on our usual walk but to stay inside instead. I was watching TV and holding the baby when I heard a huge explosion. I felt the building sway a little, as if the foundation buckled. That was the first bombing of the World Trade Center in 1993. It killed six people and injured thousands. The snow was the only reason we weren't in the building that day. The blast was so loud that even at home in the apartment, I could feel its percussion.

There were many moments of joy in that apartment. One day when my son was three months old, we were sitting on the edge of my bed and looking at the mirrors that covered the sliding closet doors. I was holding him up and talking to him in baby talk. He looked at our reflection and giggled. It was his first laugh. I know it's awfully clichéd, but no sound before or since has ever made me so happy.

In general, however, things weren't great. My life had gone from being totally focused on my dreams and my future to taking care of a newborn and all of the responsibility that entails. You are never fully prepared to be a parent, no matter how much you think it out. But only an optimistic child at twenty years old would think she could pull this off while simultaneously being a performer. What a dummy! In the back of my brain, I felt like I was letting everyone down and not living up to anyone's expectations.

Things were strained with Tommy and me. There was just a lot of pressure. He worked hard to support his new wife and baby, and I'm sure he was unhappy. I don't think this was something he saw himself doing. We were all trying to do the right thing, but sometimes the "right thing" is possibly the wrong thing.

Marriage is tough enough when you're responsible, have a steady income, and you're a well-developed human being. I was twenty years old and temperamental. Growing up, I had learned some bad habits about how to treat people. Sometimes I wasn't very nice to Tommy. No one was ever violent, but there were a lot of arguments. I was overwhelmed and unhappy, so I would pick fights with him for no reason other than to get attention. I knew no other way to communicate my frustrations.

I feel like my marriage came apart because of me, not

because of anyone else. I can take responsibility. I knew I was a good mom. I thought I was adult enough to be a wife and a mother, but really I wasn't. Tommy bore the brunt of that. It was this constant pressure, and it was hard for both of us to take.

We broke up when my son was a little more than eighteen months old. I came out of a divorced home. I did what I knew, which was to take my son and leave.

We moved out of our apartment and back into Renee's up in Tudor City. Looking back on it and talking with my mother, I think I probably should have been treated for postpartum depression after my son was born. I just felt incredibly over-whelmed with a sense of anxiety. I had stopped eating and by the time I moved in with my mother, I was very thin.

Once I got to Renee's, I became even thinner. I had thought enough to get out of my marriage, but I had no plan after that. The yawning expanse of my uncertain future seemed like it was going to swallow me whole. I had no job, no career, a child to take care of, a ruined marriage, and I was twenty-one years old. I felt doomed.

Renee, of course, loved me and her grandson. But she was not happy with how things turned out. "You know, Erika, you should have thought this out," she would say to me. "You let me down. Everything I told you, all of my stories about being a young mother, meant nothing." Thank God she was kind enough to let me move in. We ruined her life for a while.

I was talking to my mother on the phone recently. She reminded me of the sweatpants I wore every day for a month when I first moved into her apartment after my divorce. They were dark gray, and my mother said I would take them off only to wash them and put them back on. I showered and everything, but I couldn't bring myself to wear anything other than that one pair of worn-out gray sweatpants.

When we talked about it recently, Renee said, "I was really worried about you, because I would look at you and see that you were really thin. You were caring for this child, but I could see that you were totally panicked."

Now that I was out of my marriage, I also made another big change. I went to my mother's hairstylist friend and had him cut off all of my long blond hair. I had it cut short, just like Mia Farrow in *Rosemary's Baby*. I think women cut their hair in times of change. When it was done, I felt brand-new.

One of my friends said, "Why did you cut off all your power?"

I thought, *Who am I, Samson? Did I totally just cut off all my power?* But he was right, I kind of did. I was definitely looked at differently than when I had blond hair cascading down to my waist. People see a different type of woman, and they react differently. I can tell you one thing: I wasn't going to be welcome back at the go-go bars in Jersey with this new cut. With my new hair came a totally different persona. Before, I was the ingenue. Now I was just a minivan away from becoming a soccer mom. It changed the way I saw myself.

Picking myself up and trying to piece myself back together went on for a while. I would go on auditions and wouldn't get the parts. I would have to have my mom babysit because I didn't have any money to pay a sitter.

One time, I had done some job and left my son with my mother. When I got finished, I came home and there was blood on the back of his onesie and his hair in the back was matted down with blood. "What happened?" I asked Renee.

"Oh, he fell and cracked his head open on the corner of the dresser," she said, nonchalant.

"Did you take him to the hospital?" I asked.

"No, that's for you to do," she told me.

I immediately scooped him up, jumped in a cab, and took him down to Bellevue, which was the closest hospital to our apartment in Tudor City. The E.R. doctor who treated him asked, "Hey, buddy, how did this happen?"

"I'm just really stressed out," my son replied, totally dead-pan. Wonder where he'd heard that? Thank God the doctor had a sense of humor and laughed along with me.

My stress came from being in a vicious circle, a no-win situation. I could not continue at this pace, in this city, on this track, and ever expect anything to change. I knew I would never get ahead, never make anything happen. And that's when I chose to move.

By that point, things had calmed down and Tommy and I were friendly again. I don't remember the conversation specifically when I told him I was going to move, but he was always very supportive. It was never that I was leaving our son. I told Tommy, "I'm going to go get myself situated, and once I have everything figured out, I'll be right back."

I never gave Tommy any reason not to trust me. Despite some hard times, I was always very responsible with our son and put his needs first. Even then, I frequently traveled back and forth from New York to LA. I would never be gone for too long, though I was working on establishing myself on the West Coast. Putting my son first was what moving was all about. If I was going to take care of him and provide the future for him that I wanted, I knew that I had to get away and find a better life and a more sustainable existence for myself.

Tommy and I talked things out. He knew that I wasn't running away. I just needed a shift and I would come roaring back when I was ready. And boy, did I come roaring back.

I really loved Tommy, and I think I always will. He's still a part of my family now, and we'll be connected forever through our son. Once I got settled in LA and we were coparenting, our son couldn't put anything over on either of us. We talked all the time, and if he was punished at his father's house, he was punished at my house, too, and vice versa. We were always on the same page and respected each other's decisions. Once, when Thomas was still young, he said to me, "I don't know why you and Dad ever got a divorce. You never fight." And that was true, we never fought in front of our son. Once our marriage was over, we never had anything to fight about.

I still talk to Tommy, even after he and his mother moved out to Las Vegas in 2013. Usually we're texting about our son and his job and making sure that he's checking in with one of us and that he's always okay. He's twenty-five, but we're still nervous Nellie parents.

One time Tommy said to me, "I would like to look at my son just once and see something of me in him."

He's right, our son looks much more like his mother than his father. "Well, I guess I just have stronger genes than you," I joked.

But when it comes to personality, our son is his father's child through and through. He has the same cutting humor that his father does and that same made-in-Manhattan swagger that made me fall in love with Tommy all those years ago.

More recently, after the premiere party for my first season on *The Real Housewives of Beverly Hills*, I was in the backseat of my SUV headed home. I was in Hollywood, where my son was on patrol. I texted him to see if he was free. He responded that he was around the corner and he'd be by in a few minutes.

I told the driver to pull over on Hollywood Boulevard, right between Grauman's Chinese Theatre and the Dolby Theatre. It was about two in the morning. The Walk of Fame was totally empty and there was not a soul around. It was one of those cold, foggy winter nights that make LA look even more like a film noir than it already does.

A minute later, out of the darkness emerges a shape walking toward the car. It was like a phantom coming out of the night. "Oh, it's the police," the driver said, a bit concerned. It was my son in uniform.

"Don't worry, I got it," I told him. As my son approached the car, I rolled down my window to say hello.

"How was the party?" he asked.

"It was good," I told him. "What are you up to?"

"You know, just working," he said. "Mom, I think what you're doing is great. I just want you to know that I'm proud of you."

When I moved to California, I always knew that my son would eventually come out and live with me. Little did I think it would be under these circumstances, with me living this insane life and him a grown man on the police force. If you ever see me in an alley in Hollywood talking to a cop, know that everything is just fine. There have been quite a few men in my life, but there will never be one more special than him.

6

THINKING GLOBALLY

New York is a brutal bitch. When I got to the city in 1989 at age eighteen, I wasn't prepared for what making it in show business was really all about. I'm not saying I fell off a turnip truck, but still I wasn't ready for the pace of New York City.

I was forced to grow up quickly. It was such an adjustment from the South. In the Big Apple, everyone is constantly on the go, and no one—especially casting directors and talent agents—has any time for anyone. I wasn't expecting them to roll out the red carpet, but I didn't anticipate an abrupt slap in the face, either.

I had taken more dance classes than I could count. I had some experience in commercials as a kid. And I'd had a great performing arts education that honed my singing, dancing, and acting chops. What I didn't have was a clue. In high school, the focus was on the craft, not on the business of how to find a manager and agent, or join the Screen Actors Guild, or any of the logistics of becoming successful. Looking back on my education, the practical side of performing arts was definitely missing. If by the time we all graduated we had learned how to network into a job, it could have been a big game changer.

I started looking for work the only way I knew how—by pounding the pavement. Like every other wannabe performer, I'd check all the trades and go to anything that seemed like it might be a good fit. One audition that didn't seem like a fit was when my girlfriend Justine tried to get me to go with her to the open audition for the *In Living Color* Fly Girls at the Palladium. I didn't think I was right for that show, but one girl on the stage that day who *was* right for it is named Jennifer Lopez.

The New York audition scene was brutal no matter what time of year it was. Any aspiring actress has to look like whatever part she's auditioning for. If it's a commercial, she needs to look clean, perky, and cute. If it's a sexy or pretty role, she wants to be that fresh-faced girl who can land a leading man. I couldn't show up to any of these auditions looking like I had just rolled out of a Times Square Dumpster. Even at eighteen, I needed money to look good.

I was living with my mother on the Upper West Side and would take the subway to get around. God knows I didn't have the cash for cabs. In the summer I was walking around in the heat. It's boiling underground in a subway station that smells like rodent and sewage stew. By the time I arrived at auditions, I would be such a wrecked, sweaty mess that I could barely focus on getting the gig.

In the wintertime, it wasn't any better. That wind would just cut me in half. I would rush, shivering, from the subway to whatever building was holding the audition. I'd always look like shit, with my red, runny nose, watering eyes, and dry skin from the apartment radiator. In either season, it was like a setup for failure.

When I look back on it I wonder what the fuck did I think I was doing? Only an eighteen-year-old child with big, stupid dreams would attempt this. You'd have to be the most hopeful (and maybe naive) person to think that this was ever going to work.

I didn't get the chance to go to college, so I made my New York experience kind of like my college—getting out there, socializing, auditioning, getting work, not getting work. Even the experience dancing in go-go bars in Jersey was educational. It taught me a lot about people, both inside and outside of business. When people refer the school of hard knocks, I know exactly what they're talking about. I graduated from it *summa cum laude.*

I did have some successes, though. I went to a lot of auditions for all-girl groups, which were popular at the time. Think less the Spice Girls and more like Exposé. One of my first jobs at eighteen was singing with a group called The Flirts when one of their members was on a leave of absence. They had a hit with the song "Jukebox (Don't Put Another Dime)" and there was always a three-girl lineup, but it changed a bit. I filled in to record a couple of tracks with them.

I didn't think much of the people who managed the group. Still, I was excited to have the work. We were recording at Quad Studios, which is top of the line (and would later become infamous for being the place where Tupac Shakur was first shot).

The other two girls were Trish and Tracy. Trish was a beautiful blond singer/songwriter. We spent a lot of time together and became close friends. Later, she and Tracy were both bridesmaids at my wedding.

Tracy had a degree from the London School of Economics. She was very bright, so I have no idea why she was messing around with this group. She was from a wealthy family, and her stepfather owned a huge estate in Southampton called Cryptomeria. I knew it was fabulous because it had a hedge maze.

Former New York mayor Michael Bloomberg purchased it in 2011.

Anyway, Trish, Tracy, and I would go out there in the summer and hang around for a special treat. We even did a photo shoot for the group when we were visiting once. Tracy's stepfather, a big shot in the financial industry, told me, "Erika, if you ever do anything, make sure you think globally." Remember, this was the eighties. Greed was good.

Here I was, a skinny little kid in New York trying to make my showbiz dreams come true, and he's telling me to think globally. I wasn't thinking past next month's rent. However, when it came time to name my business and we wrote up the incorporation papers, I told Tom I wanted to name it EJ Global.

"Why Global?" he asked me.

"Because Tracy's father told me back in the eighties that if I ever did anything, to make sure it was global," I explained.

"Okay, Erika. Yeah," Tom replied.

I can remember being in the recording booth with The Flirts for the first time, really having to pull out some clean vocals. I worked through not being able to hit notes, not being able to hear properly, and bad timing. It was nerves more than anything, but it felt really good when I got it right. I enjoyed those days a lot.

A few months later, I was walking by a record store. I heard the song "Danger" that we had recorded coming out of the shop. The weird thing was that I only heard Trish's vocals. It's like they didn't use anything from me or Tracy. That sucked, because I know I sang the hell out of the pre-chorus.

About a decade later, while driving my car in Los Angeles, I heard another track we recorded. It was on a throwback show on KRRL, 92.3 The Beat. I called the radio station and asked where they had gotten the recording because I wanted a copy for myself. I told them I sang on the track they just played, and they put me right through to the DJ.

"Hey, what was the name of that Flirts song you just played? I'm one of the singers on it," I told him.

"Really?" he replied. "Do you want to come back and be on our oldies show?"

Oldies show? I wasn't even thirty! I was slightly insulted.

I also worked with another three-girl group called the I-Dolls. I got to fill in when one of the girls was out. (Maternity leave? Visa dispute? Prison? I don't remember.) I never recorded with them, but we did live gigs all over New York, even at really big, iconic venues like Red Zone and Roseland Ballroom. Sadly, both of those stages have since been razed to make way for luxury condo buildings.

Both of these groups were already formed by the time I

showed up on the scene. It was very clear I was just stepping in for somebody who was away, and that was fine with me. I needed a job and this was a great way to get in and meet people and do some things. Most important, it was a chance to do what I loved most and had trained to do: perform.

I also booked a few acting gigs in New York. One of my first was on the very first episode of this tiny little TV show that no one ever heard of called *Law & Order*. This was in 1990 with the original police officers: George Dzundza and a pre–Mr. Big Chris Noth.

The episode is called "Prescription for Death." It was "ripped from the headlines" of the case of Libby Zion, an eighteen-year-old girl who died from cardiac arrest in the emergency room. Overworked intern physicians had given her a prescription drug that caused an adverse reaction to an antidepressant she was taking.

I played Suzanne Morton, the first person ever to die in an episode of *Law & Order*. (This wasn't the pilot of the series, but it was the first episode to air.) John Spencer, who went on to play Leo McGarry on *The West Wing*, played my character's father, who insists on an investigation after I die. Pretty much the same things happened to my character that happened to Libby Zion, except that the doctor in charge of my character was accused of being drunk on duty instead of overworked.

I got a big death scene on screen, but for all of my hard work, I'm not even on the episode's IMDb page *or* its Wikipedia page. Of course, since *Law & Order* still airs around the clock on cable, occasionally people will recognize my bit part and send me pictures of my scenes on social media. How they recognize my much younger face, I'll never know.

A few years later, I appeared once again on *Law & Order*. They resurrected me, this time as a crack addict. I don't think I even had any lines this time, but fans will still recognize me when it replays on cable. I can't believe *Law & Order* cast me twice as a woman on drugs. What are they trying to tell me?

After we got divorced, I put my career on hold for a bit. A year later, I was back on the audition circuit. Once again, I was trying to get my career off the ground.

I auditioned for an independent movie called *Alchemy*, and I got the part. My character was married to an artist who was having an affair with another artist who looked like me. He died, and she knew about me, but I didn't know about her. She sought me out, and we became friends. It was a fun role, but it was a bit of a stretch for me. I don't think I was mature enough. Yes I was a mom at that point, but to play someone who has lost a husband . . . Frankly, I'm a good actress, but not that good.

What I remember the most about it is that we filmed in Delaware, of all places. It was fucking gorgeous. This was right before Halloween, so the pumpkins were out and the leaves had turned, but it was still warm. I remember it was just so beautiful. The movie only ever played the Hamptons Film Festival, but I really enjoyed making it.

I was also in this tacky gangster movie called *Lowball*, which one of my friends made. He basically wrote a small part for me and asked if I wanted to be in it, and I said yes. I played the wife of a drug-addicted police officer. Apparently, in the early nineties, all anyone wanted to make movies or TV shows about was drugs! It was my friend's first feature. The movie wasn't that bad, but the set was chaotic, like no one knew who was in charge.

Like that of any performer struggling in New York, my early career was a litany of near misses, tons of rejection, and occasional quiet encouragement. Juliet Taylor, the well-regarded casting director, would always have me come in to read for parts, though I didn't get any of them.

Another casting director was always on the hunt for my big break. He would say to me, "This part is just not right, but I'm going to keep looking and I'm going to give you a job one day."

I would hear no over and over, and it was hard. Then

I would get a job and think, *Okay, it's working out.* Then I wouldn't get anything for months. I'd go out for a million auditions and a million dance calls, and then some other girl would get the part. I would be frustrated all over again. As human beings, we want at our core to feel acceptance, love, and acknowledgment that we're on the right path. We want confirmation. I didn't have to get every job, but I needed small victories along the way to keep prodding myself in the right direction.

I felt like the powers that be were keeping me offstage. It was horrible. I had to continuously remind myself why I chose my art and why I loved it. Why I chose to navigate this incredibly difficult and brutal business. I did it because I loved the work, the artistic process, the connection. I loved doing it so much that when I didn't get to do it, my spirit was slightly crushed.

Looking back, the entertainment business is for the birds. Striking it big is like winning the lottery and often makes as little sense. As we all know, talent doesn't always equal success. I've watched as some of the most beautiful voices, the best dancers, and the most incredible actors lost parts to others who didn't seem as deserving. I would never begrudge anyone their success, but I know the process of constant rejection can be hard for everyone, even the biggest stars on the planet.

After being told no for so many years, I started to wonder what I was missing. Looking back, I finally know the answer. The missing key was a sense of self. I didn't have the maturity and New York was teaching me these things. I was so full of anxiety, anger, and frustration from constant auditioning, looking for work, and questioning myself. It wasn't great at the time, but the grinder of New York was exactly what I needed. Without it, I would never have found the confidence and maturity I needed to really blossom later in life.

I really think everyone should try living there for a few years when they're young and resilient. It will teach them a lot about themselves, their character, and whether they really have the drive that it takes to turn their ambitions into reality.

After the birth of my son, things got even harder for me professionally. My mom would babysit for me, because I didn't have any money to pay a sitter. I was a woman with a high school education who didn't know anything other than the performing arts. I would go on auditions, and I wouldn't get the part. I had a son to take care of. I couldn't just switch gears and become an unpaid intern somewhere. I couldn't afford to work some dead-end entry-level job. Like at every point in my life, when I hit a wall doing things the traditional way, I found my own way to do things.

Moving to LA was both the hardest and the gutsiest decision I have ever made. It was difficult to be apart from my son even for a short time. But I knew the only hope he had of living the life he deserved was for me to take this incredible risk. I knew our future wasn't in New York.

Once settled in LA, I returned to New York regularly. When I became financially stable, my son became bicoastal. He would spend summers, spring break, and alternate Christmases and Thanksgivings with me.

While my son was with my ex-husband, my mother, and my ex's mother in New York, I was furiously building our future in Los Angeles. This was not some hasty decision. It was much discussed and planned out.

Neither was this move about finding a rich man to support my son and me, no matter what some haters are bound to say. There are more billionaires in Manhattan than in any other city in the world. If that's what I was searching for, I could have stayed right at home.

Even as I struggled, I always took solace from something a casting director once told me. He said, "You have a big enough personality that one day producers will say, 'Go get me someone exactly like Erika.' Don't change your voice, don't change your look. There's something so individual about you. No one has what you have, and someday everyone will want it. But that day is a long time away, and it's going to be very hard to get there."

Turns out, he was right about everything.

7

THE LITTLE GENERAL

*W*hen I announced to my family that I was moving to LA, everyone was supportive. But no one was as supportive as my grandmother Ann. I always called her Gramby. "Grandmother" was a struggle for me when I was very young, and "Gramby" is the sound that came out, and it just stuck.

I flew from New York down to Atlanta, and Gramby bought me a used red Toyota Celica convertible. She agreed to drive across the country with me. We went to AAA and got the route all mapped out for us. We spent four days driving across the country with the top down. It was one of the best trips of my life. We talked for four days straight and never turned on the radio once. It was the first time we'd been alone together since I was a kid.

We would stop and do all of that corny shit on the side of the road that you encounter on Route 66. We stopped by the giant meteor crater in Arizona and spent a night in Vegas before making the final leg to Los Angeles. Those stops hinted at the new life I was headed toward in LA—as deep, alien, and unknowable as that crater; as neon tinted and risky as Vegas.

Gramby had the faith that I could pull it off, though. She knew I was resilient and that I could manifest whatever vision of the future I had. She knew I was tough. Hell, she was the one who made me so tough.

When we arrived in LA, she helped me find my first apartment in Hollywood before she flew back home to Atlanta. In those early years, Gramby would come out and visit me from time to time. My apartment was small, but cute. She would share the bed with me. I remember one time I had a big audition while she was there. It was strangely rainy for LA and we sat inside and she ran lines with me all afternoon. When we drove over to the audition, it was just like the old days when she would cart me all around Atlanta to auditions, dance classes, and rehearsals.

She was so supportive of me because she had taken a big leap into the unknown, just like I was doing. My grandmother grew up in a rural town in South Carolina. She and her sister wanted to get out and find opportunity in the big city. As teenagers, they made their way to Savannah, Georgia. From there, they rode the Nancy Hanks train line to Atlanta, where they lived in a boardinghouse.

She worked running the bookkeeping and accounting machines for companies like A&P and Kraft. Ann was quite the clotheshorse back then. She shopped at a fancy boutique called Joseph's. She was such a good customer, they would call her when they got new shipments in.

My grandmother met my grandfather when they were both in Atlanta. She rode the bus every day to work with a woman named Kay. Kay was married to my grandfather's older brother, Harold. She brought Ann along for a double date with her husband and his brother and the rest, as they say, is history.

My grandfather Hollis was a handsome, quiet, and stoic man. The few times he told me about his childhood, the stories were harrowing. He grew up poor in Decatur, Georgia, during the Depression. One month, all they had to eat was peaches. Sometimes his mother would wait until nightfall and then go to the neighbor's house, where she would steal tomatoes out of their garden to feed her family.

Hollis had four siblings, and his youngest sister died of diphtheria when she was two. His father never forgave himself for not getting her to the doctor in time to save her. He became a raging, abusive alcoholic who would disappear for months at a time. He told me that once his father had been gone for weeks and then showed up drunk, knocking on the front door to ask if that was where he lived. Unfortunately, it was.

One hot summer evening, while my grandfather and the family were sitting around having dinner, his father pulled out a gun and started pointing it at each of them.

"I'm going to kill all y'all tonight," he told them, pointing the gun.

Everyone got up and ran from the table—everyone except my grandfather. He just sat in his chair and kept eating his dinner. "Why aren't you leaving?" his father asked him.

"You're not going to kill anyone," he said. He was used to his father terrorizing the family. His father stared at him menacingly for a minute and then laughed, put the gun away, and started eating again. The two of them sat there in silence and finished their meals.

My grandfather only had a sixth-grade education. His father was a plumber and taught Hollis and Harold the trade. They had to quit school and start working to support the family when their father couldn't any longer.

Harold and Hollis started their own plumbing business, but Harold wanted to spend their money while Hollis did all the work. They dissolved that partnership and my grandfather struck out on his own. He did the plumbing and my grandmother ran the business, taking care of billing, invoices, the books, and everything else a small business needs. They never got rich, but they did very well for themselves. My grandfather supported a lot of people and he never complained about doing it.

Ann was a small blond woman with icy blue eyes and very pale skin. She was maybe five feet tall, but she had an aggressive personality and was domineering. We all called her "The Little General," because that is how she ruled her house. Not following her orders would cost you. Her house was always spick-and-span, her yard manicured within an inch of its life.

After she died, I consulted with Tyler Henry, a clairvoyant on the show *Hollywood Medium*. He could feel her presence. "This woman is going to be heard or else!" he told me. Even in death, my grandmother was trying to get her own way, because she honestly thought it was the best way. Ann was always bossy, but she had a southern charm about her, too. Even when she was barking orders, it didn't seem rude. However, everyone knew that she had her particularities and they had better be obeyed. She would try to boss my grandfather around, too. But he would just keep quiet and do whatever he wanted, regardless.

Ann had my mother when she was twenty-five, and she had another daughter two years later. She was really hard on those girls. My mother says that Ann's perfectionism was oppressive.

They had to take two baths a day, were never allowed to sit on their beds, and they had to look and act perfect all the time or else face their mother's disapproval. She said they were sometimes allowed to have Popsicles in the summer, but they had to eat them in the bathtub in case they dripped.

My grandmother didn't really have much respect for her daughters and had seen them mess up a lot. Frankly, she thought they were stupid because she had bailed them out of foreclosures, missed car payments, divorces, and all sorts of other trouble so many times—even when they were adults.

It was always different with me, though. I was unequivocally my grandmother's favorite. She and I communicated on a much different level. I was not her child, so I think she was somewhat softer with me than she was with her girls. I was the only person who wasn't afraid of Ann. When I was little I told her, "Don't talk to me like that, because I'm not going to take it from you." I think she saw a lot of herself in this independent child who was not going to be bossed around.

I could be just as defiant as my grandmother. I started cussing when I was five and have always had a mouth like a sailor, even though no one else in my family spoke like that. She would hit me with a belt to try to knock the bad words out of me. It never worked. I just kept running my mouth, no matter how many beatings I took. Eventually, my grandmother gave up and let me say whatever I wanted.

I wasn't exempt from beatings, though. If I talked back, tried to sass her, or didn't do something she told me to, she would still get that belt out. Sometimes if we were outside, she would get a switch and light up the back of my legs. This was the South. Back then, that is how they raised kids.

In my entire life, we only got in one huge fight. My grandmother had a big backyard, and in the middle of the lawn, there was a fishpond with flowers around it. On the side of the pond, there was a small stone statue of a little boy fishing. You could even put a little fishing pole in his hand and have the line go into the water. In the wintertime, she knitted him custom hats and scarves to keep him warm.

One day when I was in middle school, I was playing in the yard with my two young cousins. One of them pushed the statue into the water, and it broke. I wasn't there when it happened, but they blamed it on me.

My grandmother accused me of pushing it into the pond. I didn't do it, and I was ferocious about defending myself. "I know you did it and you're not admitting it," my grandmother said.

"I can't believe you would even say that," I said. "How dare you talk to me like that. You know that I have been nothing but honest with you my entire life, and for you to sit here and say something to me like that is devastating. How dare you."

"Well, I don't understand why you can't take responsibility for it. They told me you did it," she said.

"Oh great. So, you're just going to believe a couple of liars over me?" I asked her.

I thought she and I were going to come to blows because of this little fucking statue. We were up in each other's faces, going at it like street fighters.

My grandmother was used to everyone backing down from her, but I absolutely refused.

It got so heated, Renee finally came out into the yard. "The two of you need to calm down," she said, not helping at all.

"Fuck you, too," I said. "You stay out of this. This is between us."

That fight really damaged my relationship with my grandmother for a time. I thought, *How could you do this? I've been nothing but honest with you. You and I are so close. You're believing someone else over me.*

One of my cousins eventually confessed to the unforgivable crime of murdering the little fishing boy. My grandmother said to me, "I am very sorry. I apologize."

"I am still very angry that when I came to you and told you

I didn't do it, you chose not to believe me. You took their side and didn't hear me out," I said. Now I was the one not letting *her* off the hook. As with all things, we eventually got over it. But it still gets me heated now to think about that argument.

I spent a ton of time with my grandmother when I was growing up. She would drop me off at dance class and pick me up from rehearsals. We would shop together, buy patterns to make costumes, and she would wait for me at Saturday morning dance company. We would garden and play with our animals together, and go to their lake house and spend afternoons on the water fishing. In high school when I would cut class, I wouldn't be riding around smoking in the back of cars with a bunch of bad boys. I'd go hang out at my grandmother's house. She'd always tell me not to, but I think she was glad I was there.

Gramby was very creative and resourceful. She always won "Yard of the Month" at the garden club. She would pick up the most raggedy furniture from the side of the road and take it home and reupholster it and make it absolutely beautiful. She made incredible draperies, too. She was an excellent seamstress who could make a pattern for a dress out of newspaper. She and my grandfather always had projects going. They would buy houses, fix them up, and sell them. They were flipping houses long before HGTV had made it an entertainment staple.

When I was fifteen, we went to Belgium for a high school

trip and she flew out to meet me. Recently I found a note I left for her in our hotel room to greet her. A few days later, we went to Paris along with the rest of the class. She took me to see *Le Lido*, the famous Parisian cabaret with women in ornate costumes. It was the same show I was captivated by as a child after Renee saw them in Vegas and brought home the program.

Even though I got beaten when I misbehaved, I could do no real wrong in my grandmother's eyes. Even when I was off the mark, she would tell me calmly, "You know you're wrong, don't you?"

"Yes I do," I would say.

"Okay then," my grandmother would relent, happy that I knew the score.

She never let me off the hook, but for whatever reason, she never crucified me like she did with her two daughters. She would even consult me sometimes before making decisions, something she never would have done with my mother or my aunt.

After I moved away from Atlanta, I used to talk on the phone to my grandmother every day for about an hour, just catching up and chitchatting.

Eventually, things started to change for my grandmother. I first noticed something was amiss with her handwriting. She always had the most perfect penmanship, but it was getting sloppier and sloppier. Then there started to be small money mistakes: late payments, forgetting to pay some bills entirely.

Once, my son and I were visiting and she was driving us home in her minivan. We were going down these dark country roads, which are so rural that they all look the same. "Erika," she said, "I forgot how to get home."

"Do you want me to drive?" I asked, sensing she was starting to panic. She said yes, and I got into the driver's seat. Wherever we were, my phone wasn't getting any service, so that wouldn't help. "Okay, Ann," I said. "I don't know where the fuck we are."

"I don't, either," she said.

"All right. Which way do you *think* is home?" I asked. We started driving in that direction and eventually found a landmark I recognized. From there, I was able to figure it out. But that experience crystalized that something was really wrong with her. I'd never seen her so unsure and scared in my life.

She later went to the doctor and was diagnosed with Alzheimer's. She had been trying to keep her deteriorating health from the rest of us. Ann's mother had died of Alzheimer's disease. She had seen firsthand what this cruel disease would do. She knew what she was in for, and this knowledge made her both terrified and secretive. She would suffer with the disease for ten years before she died in 2014.

We still talked on the phone every day, but her personality started to change. She'd get mood swings. She'd be perfectly fine one moment, but then suddenly be scared or upset. She started to get oddly paranoid about my safety and that of my son.

A few years after my grandmother's diagnosis, my grandfather Hollis broke his hip. He was later diagnosed with stage-four stomach cancer. When he got the results back from the doctor, it was clear that he had been suffering in silence for quite some time. He didn't want to take the focus off of my grandmother and her needs.

Renee moved in with her parents to help take care of them when they were both sick. Eventually, my grandmother had to be placed in a home. She got thrown out of the first home for fighting. She said that another one of the patients pushed her, so she pushed right back. That was just like Ann.

In the new home, things could still get rough. Once I was visiting her during lunch and she yelled at another woman in the room, "Stop looking at me like that!"

"Ann, what are you doing?" I asked. "She's not doing anything."

"I don't like the way she's looking at me, Erika. Tell her to stop."

I couldn't convince her the woman didn't mean anything by it. My grandmother was as small, tough, and vocal as a Chihuahua.

In 2010, my grandfather died. By that time, my grandmother was rarely lucid and we never told her that he died. I don't think that she would have understood and it wasn't worth putting her through that pain. When she would ask for him, everyone would tell her that he was at work. Eventually, she stopped asking about him altogether.

The worst part of the disease was when my grandmother couldn't speak anymore. I would go visit her and hold her hand as she lay in bed, silent and mostly motionless. I would just put my head down and cry. She would simply sit there, showing no emotion. It's like the sickness had frozen her face. Sometimes she would gently squeeze my hand. I took that as a sign of comfort, as if in those moments she was lucid.

The year before my grandmother died, my mother called to wish me a happy birthday.

"I'm here with your grandmother," she said over speakerphone.

"Hi, Gramby," I said.

"She just raised her hand and waved at the phone," my mother said.

That was the most acknowledgment I could get, but it was enough.

It finally got to the point where my grandmother stopped eating, drinking, and swallowing. My mother called me, and I went down to Georgia to be with the two of them.

My grandmother was a conservative Protestant. She always forced my mother to play hymns like "How Great Thou Art" on the piano so she could sing them. She was an awful singer, but she would sing loud and with conviction anyway. The Lord was gonna hear her, honey. She also listened to those hellfire-and-brimstone preachers on TV and would even send them money occasionally. But she and my grandfather brought me up to love everyone and not to hate people or believe some of the other harmful things those preachers taught.

I would always ask, "How can you listen to this bullshit?"

I was the only one in the family raised Catholic, thanks to my stepfather. She would always ask, "How can *you* pray to Mary with these Catholics?"

When we were planning her funeral, we found the most gorgeous burial ground. It was on the grounds of a monastery we would always pass on the way from my grandparents' house to their lake house.

They place the body in what is essentially a wicker basket and bury it in the ground to decompose naturally. We filled my grandmother's basket with flowers and placed my grandfather's ashes in there as well, so the two of them could always be together.

On an episode of *The Real Housewives of Beverly Hills*, I visited her grave with my mother. Some viewers were confused because it looked like we were in a park. It's in a thousand acres of permanently protected wetlands in Conyers, Georgia, in the Honey Creek Woodlands. Instead of a traditional cemetery, the bodies are buried under trees, near streams, and in unspoiled nature. Rather than large headstones or monuments, there are only small grave markers that won't spoil the natural beauty of the place.

The kicker is that although it's a nondenominational burial ground, it's overseen by the Benedictine Monks at the Monastery of the Holy Spirit. I got the last laugh on Gramby, because she'll be spending eternity in the care of a bunch of Catholics.

I miss and think about her every day. She was really the most influential person in my life. I wish she were here to witness Erika Jayne's journey and talk to me about *Housewives*. She would have the best take on it and the whole circus would make her die laughing. She'd say something like, "Oh no, Erika.

This is what's really going on. Watch out for *this* woman. Keep your eye out for *that* one. But *this* other one, you can trust."

It's sad that she'll never get to see the show or my continued success, my son's, and that of the people she loved. But everyone goes through this. It is the natural order of things. As sad as this makes me, it could have been a lot worse for us. She was always the person I was closest to, from when I was a toddler and we were both calling bullshit on all the fools in our lives. I learned a lot from the Little General. I'll always miss being her most faithful lieutenant.

8

KNOWLEDGE IS A POWERFUL APHRODISIAC

*W*hen I moved to Los Angeles, I was twenty-five years old. All I owned was the red convertible my grandmother and I drove across the country in and a trunkful of clothes. I found a cute one-bedroom apartment in Hollywood on Orange Drive, below Sunset Boulevard. I went to Ikea and bought the basics: a bed, a kitchen table, and some dishes and utensils.

My life was bare bones, and I was very content with that. I didn't feel as if I needed a whole of bunch of stuff. This was an interesting time. I felt very excited about the possibilities of a new city, getting a fresh start, and working to achieve my career aspirations.

Recently my son and I were driving by my first place. I pointed it out and said, "That was my first apartment in LA."

"Mom," said my son, who is now a police officer in LA, somewhat in shock. "This is kind of a fucked-up area."

"You think it's bad now?" I said. "Imagine what it was like twenty years ago when I moved here!"

When I lived in that apartment, a part-time pimp/crack dealer lived across the way. Retired 18th Street Gang members lived next door. They were all cool with me, though. They didn't give me any problems. The building was very cute with a lemon tree out front. It had the fifties-style architecture that made it seem like old Hollywood. Even the apartment itself had quaint little details, like shelving built into the closets, that gave it some warmth.

As soon as I had moved in, I immediately started going to every audition I could find. I had an agent, but it was a boutique agency. It closed within my first year and a half in Los Angeles. None of the other agencies were clamoring to represent me, so I was left to my own devices.

The audition circuit in LA was totally different from what I was used to. In New York, you would sweat your makeup right off your face on the crowded subway and then ruin your hair walking through the blustering wind. In LA, you got into your car and had air-conditioning. The biggest problem was maybe you struggled to find a place to park or got delayed by traffic, but that was it. You were able to arrive pretty much camera ready.

There are also two different types of actors. In New York, they're mostly theater people doing "legit acting," as they call it. In LA, it's TV and film actors, which is a very different look and feel. It's a very subtle way of acting, because you're performing for the camera, not the cheap seats in the back of a theater. Also, the casting directors in New York have less than zero time for you. LA is just as Machiavellian, but they are fake nice on the outside. You know they're gonna fuck you over, but you can't quite tell when, where, or how.

I found Los Angeles just easier on the whole—as a place to live, operate, and do well. New York is very difficult. I *could* do it, but I didn't want to. New York requires a completely different mind-set and philosophy.

In New York, I always felt a little like a fish out of water. But from the moment I arrived in LA, I had a feel for the city. As hard as it might be to believe, I've never been lost in Los Angeles. I just instinctively knew my way around. And I knew that LA was where I needed to be professionally and that my life would open up there. I could tell that I would live here for a very long time. I knew that as hard as it was to temporarily be away from my son while he went to school in New York, eventually he would make his life out here with me. I could feel my future in Los Angeles, in a way that I never could when I was in New York.

On the outside, my move looked crazy. But to me it made sense. I could see the endgame.

I got some small parts. I was a guest star on a short-lived cop show called *High Incident* that starred Blair Underwood. I played a diner waitress with the improbable name of Cindy Butterworth. Cindy filed for divorce from her husband, who got so upset that he took her, and everyone else in the diner, hostage. Yeah, I wasn't going to win any Emmys, but at least I was booking some parts.

In that first year, I was mostly paying the rent by working retail. I worked at a small boutique that sold women's contemporary clothing. I started in the Beverly Center and then moved over to their location in the Century City Mall, which is still there. I never cared for sales because the pay was lousy, the hours were all consuming, and it could be boring. I spent hours staring out at the vast beige expanse of the Beverly Center, waiting for my shift to end.

In the golden age of Hollywood, Chasen's was a famous restaurant opened in 1936 by comedian Dave Chasen. It was famous for serving chili and other southern staples. For many years, it was the home to the annual Academy Awards party, and it was there that Ronald Reagan proposed to Nancy. Its original location closed in 1995, but in 1997 the original owners' grandson reopened in a different spot at 246 N. Canon Drive. (After a short run, it closed and was replaced by Mastro's Steakhouse in 2001.)

Sharon Lee, an acquaintance of mine, was working as a cocktail waitress in the new Chasen's and said she could get me an interview. I talked to Grady Sanders, who was running the place. He asked me if I had any experience working as a cocktail waitress. I said I did, which wasn't entirely untrue. I had been a cocktail waitress for a bit after I moved on from the go-go clubs in New Jersey, but that was only a brief stint. I figured that I was a quick study and I could pick it up on the fly.

Grady gave me the job. He was an interesting character who drove a white Rolls-Royce, had a thick Texas accent, called a Heineken "Texas champagne," and was always finessing and finagling things to go his way. He's since died, and I hope he's resting in peace. He always did right by me.

The new Chasen's was two floors. The formal dining room was downstairs, and the upstairs was more like a private club. It had a private dining room and a bar, which is where I worked. The decor was dark woods with chintz drapes in jewel tones, dark greens and burgundies. There was a large, semicircular bar and a big fireplace. It was very much like a club where you would see men drinking scotch in front of paintings of fox-hunts. While there were just as many female customers, the vibe was very masculine.

All of the cocktail waitresses wore floor-length emerald-green, sleeveless turtleneck gowns. They were made out of a very comfortable stretch velvet, which doesn't sound really cute, but was actually quite elegant. I wore that every shift with a pair of very high black pumps.

I look back on the work with fond memories. Sure, there were nights where I'd rather have been anywhere else, as I served drinks to self-important people. But compared to retail at the Beverly Center, this was better by leaps and bounds. I was in a pretty place that served quality food and drinks. I was wearing an elegant gown while making decent money. At that point, I had nothing. For someone trying to put a life together in a new city, I wasn't doing too badly.

When the restaurant opened, it was doing very brisk business. We had an older, wealthier crowd local to Beverly Hills, who were nostalgic for the original Chasen's. This was a totally different place, though, even if we still served that famous Chasen's chili. I tried it once and it was good, made from a nice cut of beef. I had never been to the original location, so I couldn't tell if it was just as good, better, or total slop compared to what Ronald Reagan used to order.

Lots of doctors, lawyers, entertainment executives, and the occasional celebrity came in. I once waited on Phyllis Diller, who said, "Hey, kid, you look a little like that actress Sharon Stone." Diahann Carroll had her best gay tell me, "Ms. Carroll thinks you're very beautiful." I almost died when I waited on Debbie Reynolds. All I could think about was *Singin' in the Rain*. My heart almost stopped when I waited on Cyd Charisse. She was so beautiful, and I think she's one of the all-time greats.

There was lots of old LA dough coming through the place. There were also a lot of broke Beverly Hills wannabes, too, pretending they were still able to afford that lifestyle. They're the impossible ones who wanted everything and were so demanding, yet they never tipped and were the meanest to the waitstaff. The ones with the most money never complained. You could dump their entrées into their laps, and they would remain composed.

My best friend at Chasen's was a bartender named Randy. Much like myself, he is a blond who came from New York to LA to be an actor. He had booked a lot of commercials back when there was good money to be made in them. He worked at Chasen's, then at the Peninsula, and then all over town. He was the kind of upscale bartender who people always wanted to chill with. People would come visit him from all around the globe. Wherever he was working, they would come find him. He knew everyone in town, and everyone knew him.

There was this one customer both Randy and I hated. He would always drive his red Ferrari to the restaurant. He'd sit down at the bar, order the staff around, and treat everyone like dirt. He was the classic LA loudmouth. He didn't tip, and no one wanted to deal with him. One day, during a lunch shift, Randy and I were working together. We saw a flatbed truck pull up in front of the restaurant. We watched out the window as this guy's Ferrari got repossessed right there on Canon. Karma may be a bitch, but that afternoon her tab was on Randy and me.

Here's a friendly tip, be good to the bartender, because he sees and hears all your shit. I've been out of the scene for years now, but I knew the dirt on everybody, because my bartender friends would tell me. They knew who was coming and going, who was shacked up where with hookers, who was about to get fired, and who had just fucked some girl in the parking lot.

Randy was a great friend. We had a lot in common and could always make each other laugh, especially when we were making fun of some of the more, how can I put this, "eccentric" customers. When I was learning golf, we'd go play together on the public course. I was awful and didn't want anyone at the country club judging me. Randy was always encouraging, even though he was so much better.

The most important thing about my job at Chasen's is that I met my future husband, Tom Girardi, there. Tom is a world-renowned trial attorney and founder of Girardi & Keese, a downtown LA law firm. As a young man, Tom was the first lawyer in the state of California to win a $1 million verdict, which was for a medical malpractice suit. He is perhaps most famous for winning a $333 million case against Pacific Gas & Electric for the 650 residents of Hinkley, California. The company's practices were giving residents high rates of cancer. This is the case that inspired the 2000 movie *Erin Brockovich*, for which Julia Roberts won her Oscar. Over the years, he's won many billions for his clients in verdicts and settlements.

Tom had a small investment in the restaurant. He would be there quite often, especially upstairs near the private club where I worked. Whenever he was meeting attorneys from a different firm, a journalist for an interview, or some colleagues for a glass of wine, he would always do it at Chasen's. Tom had all of his office holiday parties and special events at Chasen's, and he would sometimes bring his adult children in with him.

Back then, Tom looked much like he does now, but twenty years younger: a dusting of gray hair, sparkling blue eyes, and the sweetest smile I had ever seen. He still had that solid build from when he was a college baseball player.

What really attracted me to him was the way that he interacted with people. This man treats everyone with respect. Whether it is the busboy, the cocktail waitress, the server, the janitor—he acknowledges everyone and looks them in the eye. He was obviously wealthy, very well educated, and at the top of his field, yet he was so kind and generous. Everyone loved Tom.

After getting to know him, I learned that he was divorced. After a year of working in the restaurant, one night I decided to slip Tom my telephone number. We were standing in front of the giant fireplace. "Did you hear I was single?" I asked.

The next day, his secretary called me and said, "Mr. Girardi would like to know if you're free to have dinner this evening."

"Absolutely not," I told her. "Tell Mr. Girardi if he wants to take me out on a date, he needs to call me himself and ask me and give me enough time to prepare." You know how men are, especially if they are successful. They expect you to drop everything right away. That's not how I work, I don't care who you are.

He did call me back himself, and he asked me out on a date like a gentleman. For our first date, we went to Ristorante Peppone, which is a little Italian restaurant on Barrington Court near the 405 freeway. (I knew Tom was allergic to garlic but did not yet know he exclusively ate Italian food or steaks.) I was wearing a tight black sweater, black pants, and black Gucci pumps. I ordered chicken Parmesan.

Tom and I have never really been apart since that night at Peppone. Since we had known each other for over a year, there was no getting-to-know-you period. I had already met all of his children and his colleagues, even though it was in my capacity as a cocktail waitress. Everything just kind of fell into place, and we gelled immediately.

Tom is thirty-three years older than me. It was always a bigger deal to everyone else than it was to either of us. All a couple really needs is to have the same life philosophy. If you see things the same way, then age, race, religion—none of that comes into play. When you want and enjoy the same things, it's more important than being born during the same presidential administration.

I have a thirst for knowledge and Tom has a wealth of it. He is a great mentor, a great teacher, and somebody I really admire. He is adventurous, loves to travel, loves to eat, and loves to have a good time. He's well read and educated. That kind of stuff is a powerful aphrodisiac.

At work, I chose to keep our relationship secret. Because number one, you don't date the customers. It just doesn't look good, especially when you're a young woman and the customer is a wealthy older man. Number two, I didn't know where this was going, so I didn't want to make a big deal of it. Number three, I know from experience, you must keep things close to the vest.

Our dating life was pretty simple. We had a great time on that first date, and he asked me out again a couple of days later. We just kept meeting up. I still worked my shifts, and Tom would still come by. It was very normal. Tom was always very busy, so we didn't have tons of time. We'd go out to dinner and then maybe out for drinks with his friends afterward.

The more time I spent with him alone, the stronger the bond between us got. Tom has this incredible twinkle in his eye and a powerful lust for life. I just fell in love with the man who talked to me about the future and my plans for life. When he spoke, he made me feel like I was the only person in the room. Heck, he made me feel like the only person in the *world*. It was inspirational.

Throughout our entire relationship, Tom inspired me to strive for something and to be ambitious. He taught me that life is good and I can achieve anything. That's not a philosophy I'd ever experienced before. Renee's views on life were much more negative. So were the views of most people in my life until then. It was always problems, problems, problems, there's never enough, men are horrible, and so on. It was about operating from a sense of lack. Tom's perspective comes from a sense of abundance. In his work, he is always bringing to light the harm that befell his clients, yet he manages only to see the good in life.

That is so attractive. I wanted to run toward it. When someone is positive, successful, loving, inspirational—I gotta tell you right now, that shit is seductive. That is more enticing to me than six-pack abs and a chiseled jawline.

Tom was excited to include me in his life and educate me about the law and what he does. If we went to dinner with another attorney and they discussed a case, they wouldn't just talk shop and ignore me. Tom would say, "Okay, Erika, listen to this. This is the case we're working on, and this is why he and I don't see things the same way."

He would explain the particulars of the situation and the laws governing it. I would become a part of the conversation, and I'd walk away knowing something about the law. More important, I would feel included and valuable to the conversation.

"What do you think, now that I've explained it to you?" he would ask.

Then both men would listen intently. I gave my opinion, and they paid the utmost attention. I found out later they were interested in a layperson's opinion of their case and its merits.

That information comes in extremely handy when presenting arguments to a jury. But I liked how it made me feel. It was incredibly seductive.

In my experience, most men are not really interested in teaching their partners shit. Rarely does a woman meet a man who will explain things to her without making it feel like he's talking down to her. Tom explains things in a way that's uplifting. It's like, "Oh, let me show you this. Let me exchange this knowledge with you." Tom would never "mansplain" something to me. He always values my intelligence, even if I wasn't educated on a particular topic of discussion.

I've always been attracted to smart, successful men. I've dated people with more money than Tom. I've dated people in more powerful positions than him. But he was someone who included me in the conversation and never took my presence for granted.

Tom loves the law. He loves to share his knowledge of it, and he wanted me to be a part of something he loved so much. He made me love it, too. I loved every minute of it. I thought it was cool. I was there to listen and soak it all up.

A few months after we started dating, I lost the lease on my apartment. I temporarily moved in with my friend Victor, who was nice enough to take me in. But that wasn't going to last forever.

*E*rika, wondering who all these fools are.

*H*ere's a picture of me at two from a scrapbook my mother kept. I'm taking this to my plastic surgeon to get those lips back.

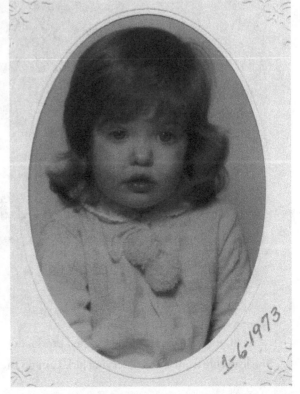

1-6-1973

$\mathcal{S}$tanding out from the pack on the far left before my first dance recital, age five.

$\mathcal{T}$he St. John the Baptist kindergarten production of *Mrs. Jingle B,* where I stole the lead role from a less deserving girl. I am on the far right, seated.

*M*e in first grade, over school and over this jumper.

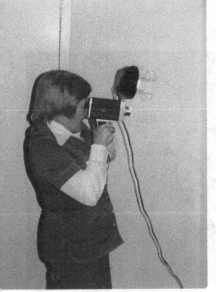

*T*his is my grandmother, Ann, filming me with her 8mm camera. She was so little she cut off all our heads in the frame.

Hollis with Anne

December 4, 1928 - July 19, 2010

*T*he program from the memorial service for my grandfather, Hollis, in 2010. He's pictured with my grandmother, Ann, who died four years later. They spelled her name wrong!

Royal Academy of Dancing

PATRON HER MAJESTY THE QUEEN   PRESIDENT Dame Margot Fonteyn de Arias, D.B.E.

8 College Avenue, Upper Montclair, N J 07043 • (201) 746-0184

CHILDREN'S EXAMINATIONS : U.S.A.

Name *Erika Chamoy*

Grade *Four*

Centre *Atlanta*

Date *14.4.83*

Report

BARRE	ADAGE
Fully stretch the knees, improve the placing of the hips.	*Take care with posture. placing of arabesque needs care.*
ALLEGRO CHARACTER STEPS	**MUSICALITY MUSIC TEST**
good elevation; now strengthen the placing. Pirouettes need great care.	*interpretation needs more practice.*
DANCE	**RESPONSE**
Rather confused, so little presentation.	*Erika shows much potential. She should practise her work, and strengthen the placing. Work well presented.*

Result *Pass Plus.*   *Heather Rice* Examiner

NO CORRESPONDENCE WILL BE ENTERED INTO RELATING TO THIS REPORT.

*M*y report card from the Royal Academy of Dancing examination. I was pissed that I was not rated "highly commended."

*M*e pulling focus in the eighth grade class photo in 1985. These are the people I wouldn't get confirmed with.

A glamour shot of Erika and Renee, NYC, 1994. *Courtesy of Ron Rinaldi*

Diciembre 6 del 78
Erika:
Espero que el
que venga de
cación.
Tu mamá
de permiso de
gar a verme. Re-
erda que aquí
queremos
ucho.
Besos.
Esther

Querida Erika:

Felices Pascuas
y Próspero
Año Nuevo

Son los deceos
de tu abelita.

Esther

A Christmas card that my paternal grandmother, Esther, who lived in El Salvador, sent me when I was seven.

Renee, my aunt Janet, and me before a night of clubbing in London, 1986. What is with this hair and these outfits?

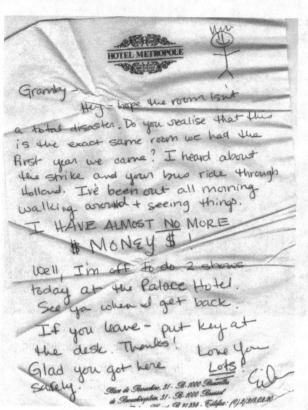

HOTEL METROPOLE

Granny—

Hey—hope the room isn't a total disaster. Do you realise that this is the exact same room we had the first year we came? I heard about the strike and your bus ride through Holland. I've been out all morning walking around + seeing things.

I HAVE ALMOST NO MORE $ MONEY $!

Well, I'm off to do 2 shows today at the Palace Hotel. See ya when I get back. If you leave — put key at the desk. Thanks! Glad you got here safely. Love You Lots!

The note I left for my grandmother when she came to meet me during a class trip to Belgium. I roomed with her instead of a classmate every year because she let me sneak out.

Putting on the Ritz circa 1990 in the apartment I shared with my first husband on 100th and Amsterdam Ave. in Manhattan.

"The Flirts," just another '80s girl group. Me at eighteen, Trish (top), and Tracy, who looks incredibly cold.

My day planner from senior year in high school where I was rehearsing for an ill-fated production of *Pippin* and performing with the Northside High School Tour Show.

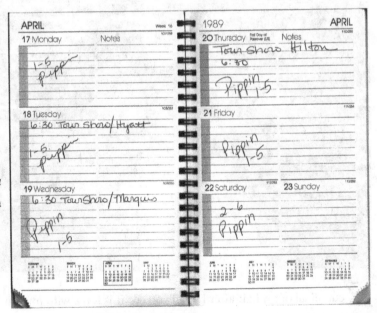

*M*y son and me, summer 1994, in downtown Manhattan. He's two and I'm twenty-two.

I cut off all of my hair after I got divorced. This is me with my son in 1995 on Catalina Island. His smile is way more adorable than my hair.

A photo a friend took of me after I first arrived in Los Angeles in 1996. Cheese, anyone? *Courtesy of David Stroud*

Tom Girardi's picture from Loyola High School in Los Angeles.

*T*om, my son, and me at another Democratic fundraiser we dragged the little guy to.

*T*om and me on a trip to Hong Kong in 2000.

*W*orking hard as a wildlife spotter on a family safari in Africa.

*M*y son and me fishing on our boat in Alaska.

*T*he original Pretty Mess Krewe after a performance at the start of the Erika Jayne project in 2009. *Courtesy of Marco Bollinger*

*M*ikey showing me how the moves are done while filming my 2010 music video for "One Hot Pleasure." But he didn't have to do it in those boots! *Courtesy of Marco Bollinger*

*G*oofing off with the boys after a gig during Gay Ski Week in 2014.

*M*ikey and me after a performance in 2014. You can tell by the looks on our faces we really needed that pivot.

*M*y assistant Laia, myself, and creative director Mikey at my first premiere party for the *Real Housewives of Beverly Hills*.

The Pretty Mess Krewe in the hot tub in Mykonos in 2016. We stayed up until dawn celebrating my forty-fifth birthday.

Coming out of my cramped trailer on the opening night of *Dancing with the Stars* in 2017.

Tom and my dog Tiago on our plane on a trip to Santa Barbara in 2015.

RHOBH girls taking a break from bickering and rehabbing a home for Habitat for Humanity in Watts.

Yolanda Hadid and me post-taping my first reunion, grabbing drinks at the Beverly Hills Hotel.

*M*y *Valley of the Dolls* meets *Stepford Wives* sit-down look for my first season of *RHOBH*.

*K*yle Richards and me in Mykonos. Yes, the one in Greece, fool. *Courtesy of Taylor James*

*B*ehind-the-scenes selfie in a big glamorous mall with Eileen Davidson and Lisa Rinna on a cast trip to Dubai.

"Where are you going to go?" Tom asked when I told him about it.

"Oh, I'll figure it out," I said nonchalantly. These things, while stressful, always have a way of working themselves out.

"You know my house is really big," Tom said. "You could leave your stuff in my garage while you look for a place, or you could just stay there while you figure things out."

"I don't know," I told him. I didn't want to jump into anything. At that point, I had only been to his house one other time when he cooked dinner for me. But after a few more weeks on Victor's couch, I reconsidered. We decided that I would live with Tom, just as friends, and I would have my own bedroom down the hall from his.

Before moving in, I got rid of all my Ikea furniture. That day at Tom's house, I just rolled up in my convertible.

"Where's all your stuff?" Tom asked.

"It's here in these trash bags," I told him as we unloaded them out of the backseat.

"All you have is a car and your clothes?"

"Yup."

"Okay. I thought you were going to have furniture and things."

"No, I don't have any of that. I got rid of it all."

"All right then," he said.

As I was thinking about what my life in that house would be like, I fully realized just how sparsely furnished it was. Tom had the basics—beds, a kitchen table, a couch—but you could tell that a man lived there alone. Here we were, two adults in this huge house. Between us, we had barely any possessions at all.

I set myself up in the room down the hall from Tom, which is the room where my son lives now. It's a large guest room with a big fireplace. Our split living arrangement was a little foolish, because every night I would sneak down the hall into Tom's bed, using him as my human body pillow. After a month, we dropped the pretense. I just moved into his bedroom.

Slowly, we started acquiring furniture—some chairs here, a bookcase there—but nothing that would blow your socks off. It was really just subsistence furniture.

We carried on with this arrangement for a few months. I was still working at Chasen's, but one night Tom said, "I think you should quit waitressing there." I agreed.

None of the other staff knew that we were dating or that I was living with Tom, so it was a surprise when I gave notice. On my last night working there, everyone was asking what my next job was going to be.

"Eh, nothing," I told them.

"Really?" my coworkers asked, confused.

Randy knew what was going on the whole time because we

were close friends and he was happy for both of us. "Erika, this is great. He really loves you, and you deserve this. You guys are cute together," he said. To get the approval of someone who knew both of us so well was very sweet.

My last night at Chasen's, I took off that stretch velvet green gown for the last time. I had been wearing it for more than a year, and it was starting to fray along the seams. I folded it up very neatly into a perfect little square (you never forget your retail skills).

I walked over to one of those industrial-sized gray rubber trash cans by the bar. I laid that green dress on top of the trash and added my pumps. It was a little funeral shrine.

Closing the lid, I walked out of that restaurant and into a whole new life.

9

GIVING THE LAYMAN'S OPINION

om and I took our relationship public. Out at the country club or some other event, I would see some of the people I used to wait on at Chasen's. It was just like, "Hey, remember me?" I always knew who was a cheap tipper, who was having an affair, who acted like an asshole, and who was actually a really cool person. But now, I was meeting these people as an equal rather than as a member of the staff. It was hilarious that I went from being the cocktail waitress in a gown to being a cocktail party guest in a much nicer gown. I was still asking the same people, "Hey, how's it going, man? How are you?" I'm sure some of them were scared, because they knew exactly what I'd seen them up to.

At first, I didn't always get a warm reception. I'm Tom's

third wife, and he is a very successful, well-known attorney. People were seeing this twenty-seven-year-old walk in with him. Immediately, everybody thought I was going to have a baby so I could lock down some of his money. They didn't know that I already had a child to take care of and was focused on doing what was right for him. *His* future was most important to me, not having another child.

When I was first on the scene, plenty of the other wives weren't especially friendly. We were socializing with lawyers and Tom's other acquaintances, so many of them knew Tom's previous wives. They weren't hostile to my face, but I would overhear, "Oh, why is she wearing that?" or, "Why is her hair cut like that?" or, "What is her motive?" Quite honestly, I think they were looking at me like, "Holy shit, am I next to be replaced?"

There were a couple of really nice, powerful, wealthy older women who befriended me. It was the wealthiest women who were the nicest. Some of them were second or third wives like me, and they had been in the same position before. The great part about having older women friends is that they've been through every part of marriage: they've been sick, healthy, broke, and wealthy. They've disciplined bad kids and dealt with mistresses. You name it, they've done it.

I was visiting with one of these women recently. She's

very wealthy and well known. She said, "You're still the same twenty-seven-year-old little girl I met many years ago. You've never changed. You've always been this way, and I'm very proud of you." At hearing that compliment, I almost started to tear up at the table.

This woman is famous in Los Angeles for wearing millions of dollars in jewelry at all times, as many of the women I was socializing with did. Early on in our relationship, I went to Tiffany and bought myself a small silver chain with a heart on it. It wasn't expensive. When Tom saw me wearing it, he got upset. "You don't buy jewelry for yourself, that's my privilege. I get to do that," he told me.

"Tom, it wasn't very expensive. It's no big deal," I told him.

"That's what I like to do. I want to buy your jewelry, I don't care that it's small," he said. I always felt that was cool of him. He's bought me a ton of beautiful stuff, which I really love. Now I wear as much as I can on *The Real Housewives of Beverly Hills* and in the cast photos. I try to sneak in everything as a reminder of our time together.

About six months after I "temporarily" moved into Tom's house in Pasadena, I got my most significant piece of jewelry. He took me out onto one of the balconies overlooking the lush backyard, got down on one knee, and asked me to marry him.

He presented me with a beautiful diamond engagement ring. Of course I said yes.

After our engagement, Tom said, "Listen, I'll buy you anything you want. I don't care what it is. You name it. But I'm not wearing a wedding band. I never have, I never will. I don't like it. It's uncomfortable. Please don't ask me to."

I agreed to his request. Listen, a wedding ring does not have magical powers. It is not going to stop anyone from doing something. Whoever thinks his or her spouse is going to magically look down at their hand and all of a sudden not make a bad decision is a fool. I don't care if Tom doesn't wear a wedding ring. He doesn't mind if I don't wear mine on occasion, either (though some people who watch the show make a big deal about it every time they spot me without it).

Neither of us ever even thought to get a prenup. It never came up. Let's be serious, Mr. Girardi knows the law so well that a prenup is not going to do shit. As any lawyer will tell you, there is always a way around a prenup, even if you think it is ironclad. Tom was going to protect himself no matter what, and what did I need to protect? The little red convertible and trash bags full of clothes I rolled up with? At the time, neither of us really thought we'd ever need one.

We were married six months later, in January. Since it wasn't a first marriage for either of us, we didn't want to make the ceremony into a big ordeal. One day, I was at home and Tom called and said, "Judge Flynn can marry us today." Judge Paul Flynn, who became famous for presiding over Snoop Dogg's 1995 murder trial, is a good friend of Tom's. He agreed to officiate.

I went down to the Gucci store and told Esther, the salesgirl I bought from all the time, I was going to get married later that afternoon. We picked out a long, silvery satin dress that was quite pretty. Tom picked me up and we went over to the LA Country Club. Judge Flynn came off the golf course and put his robe on over his golf clothes to marry us in a small reading room in the clubhouse.

Tom's best friend, Robert Baker, who defended OJ Simpson in his civil trial, was there with us to serve as a witness. Judge Flynn said to us, "I think you need two witnesses for a marriage."

"Hold on one minute," Tom said. He went into the bar looking for someone who could be our other witness. He saw Wayne Bohle, a fellow lawyer, and said, "Hey, Wayne. Erika and I are getting married. Can you come over here and be our second witness?" This was the first time I had ever met Wayne, but he sure did us a solid. Without him, Tom and I would still be living in sin.

After the brief ceremony, Tom and I got into our car. We drove over to the airplane, then flew to Vegas to have dinner that night at our favorite place. It would be just the two of us at Michael's Gourmet Room, at the now-demolished Barbary Coast Hotel. I called my grandmother from the car and told her we had gotten married. She was excited because she knew how much I loved Tom.

My grandmother especially loved Tom. When she would come to visit, she and Tom would get in his convertible and go grocery shopping at Bristol Farms. He would put one thing in the cart, and she'd take it out. "Uh-uh, you already have one of those at home," she would say.

Had she been in the cupboards taking inventory all day? How did she know what we had? Finally, I had to tell her to let him do his shopping his own way. "Gramby," I said. "This is his house, and he's spending his money. If he wants to buy a million cans of asparagus, just let him."

"But I know he already has two at the house," she'd insist.

That was my grandmother, defiant and controlling to the very end, even with Tom. They always got along, though. He found it endearing that she was so concerned about his lack of thriftiness.

Immediately, I started living Tom's life. It was a great legal education. I sat in so many meetings, dinners, and talks with the very best legal minds. I went to the U.S. Supreme Court to watch a session. A friend of ours, who was attorney general for the state of California at the time, was arguing a case. Between the huge curtains in the court and the nine justices sitting in that great room, it was truly impressive.

Tom has always been very involved in politics. We would go to the Senate to meet people and talk to them on an intimate level. This was not the kind of meet and greet where you shake a politician's hand and get a picture with him. (Yes, it's almost always a him.) No, we would have dinner with the mayor and his wife, and we'd listen to what he thinks about the city's homeless problem. We would have drinks with a U.S. senator, and she'd confide in us the problems the senators were having with the current administration. These were some great experiences.

It was a very busy and rewarding life for us. We'd be out most nights after work, socializing and attending events until around midnight. We'd drive home together and listen to murder mysteries from the thirties and forties on the radio. They were these old radio plays. We'd ride silently in the car, holding hands, trying to figure out who the killer or thief was. That was always one of my favorite rituals. I was so sad when they took those off the air.

Aside from being Tom's legal sounding board and voice

of the layperson at dinners, I served other important functions, too. At a business dinner with another couple, I would entertain the wife while Tom was trying to settle a case. I've had to do a lot of that. Since Tom does so much business in social settings, my job as his wife is to help him close the deal. I have to be charming to everyone, even when sometimes I'd rather be at home watching Oprah's *SuperSoul Sunday*.

I'm also in charge of making sure that Tom's suits are laid out. His things are hung up in the closet all paired out—each suit with a matching shirt and tie, as well as belts, socks, and shoes. I'm in charge of making sure that he has everything that he needs. That he has his particular toothpaste and his particular cologne.

I enjoy being able to do that for him. I think that it shows that I care and want him to have fewer things to worry about. Getting him ready shows that I took the time to think of him. He's not going to do it for himself, so if he walks out of the house looking crazy, that makes us both look bad. I try to make sure he always looks like a million bucks.

If something blows up around the house, do not ask Tom to fix it. Don't ask him to wash the clothes, put away the dishes, or hang up his laundry. I take care of as much of that as I possibly can. But if you want to know anything about the law or how the legal system works, he is a treasury of knowledge. He knows everything that there is to know on the subject. I can handle the rest, or else hire someone who can.

Now that I'm busier with my own career, Tom helps me out as well. He will bring home dinner when he knows I haven't eaten. If he's having a dinner meeting, he'll call me and say, "Hey, I'm at Morton's tonight. I know you're in the studio. Would you like me to bring you home a steak?"

That's what being a partner is about. It's not just about smooches or trying to look all cute and romantic in selfies. It's the most mundane things that help your other half get out there and be the best that he or she can be. Period.

I feel like women have these unrealistic expectations in marriage. As if somehow or another, Prince Charming is going to ride up on a white horse, pay all her bills, listen to all her business, and want to hang out with her and her friends. I've got news for you, honey. They don't want that. They want your support just as much as you want theirs.

It's not all sunshine and unicorns in the Girardi household. Like any couple, we can really get on each other's nerves. He can be a brat, and I can be an even bigger brat. He hates it when I talk over him, or when he hasn't completely finished saying something and I'm like, "But wait a minute, what about this,

this, and this?" I get impatient with him because he can be very long winded. He thinks I'm being bratty and pushy.

He'll respond, "If you'd let me finish, I'll answer all those questions, Erika." Sometimes I feel like he's trying to lecture me, but he always ends up giving good advice or good information. It's usually something I would have missed. Tom wants me to say everything I want to say, he just wants me to deliver it with a softer touch and to wait my turn. He wants everyone to play by the rules, like we're in a courtroom.

There's one thing that Tom has been doing for our entire relationship that drives me insane. It will keep happening as long as we're together. He'll say, "Hey, we have to go to this thing on Friday."

"Okay. What thing?" I'll ask.

"Oh, I don't know. It's like this lawyer thing."

"Well, where is it?"

"I don't know, it's on the website."

"Well, is it in a house? A restaurant? A theater? A palace?"

"Um, I think it's like a cocktail party."

We get there, and it's a formal dinner at someone's house. I'm dressed like we're going to a cocktail party. Again.

Tom says every event is "no big deal." When we get there, it's an intimate sit-down dinner with three heads of state, the pope, and Barbra Streisand. Tom can't describe it in such a way that I can prepare. For the record, my example is fictional—I have never been to dinner with the pope. I *have* been to dinner with Barbra Streisand. It was at a Clinton fund-raiser where we sat at a table of six and talked about her performances.

No matter what the occasion, Tom always says, "Just put on some lip gloss and fluff up your hair." Seriously?

I'll say to him, "You do want me to show up looking beautiful, right?"

"Yes, of course."

"Do you realize that that takes time?"

"Well, what does it take? Like forty-five minutes?"

"No, sweetheart. It takes three days."

While we can get on each other's nerves a little, we rarely have giant arguments. One of the best things Tom ever did for me was to keep me from fighting dirty. I think I learned from my mother some ways of talking to people that can be very damaging. For example, how to cut someone deeply with words. I did a lot of that in my first marriage. It always made things worse and I regret it.

The first time I ever tried that with Tom, he put a stop to it very quickly. "You don't talk like that," he told me. Notice it wasn't, "You don't talk to *me* like that." He was telling me that I mustn't say awful things to anyone, especially the people I love, no matter how justified I feel in the moment. When words leave your mouth, they're irretrievable. There is no argument for which winning justifies collateral damage. I've learned not to lash out and call names, but to explain why I'm angry or upset. Tom doesn't like screaming in our house. That's not the way to get his attention anyway. As soon as I would raise my voice, I'd already lost him.

Over time, Tom's family and my own began to meld. I even started spending holidays with him and his children from his previous marriage, and his grandchildren. What was so strange to me was that it was actually enjoyable. There were no fights breaking out, nobody was mad at someone else.

After one Thanksgiving, I called home. I said, "You know what, Renee? I was with Tom's family today, and they all get along. There wasn't any drama. What's wrong with our country-ass family? I didn't hear even once, 'Well, look at her fat ass. I never liked her. I didn't want to eat her ambrosia salad anyway.'"

What was most important to me is that Tom treated my son very well. He made it possible for me to give him the best of everything. After Tom and I were married and I had my

West Coast life figured out, my son was six. He decided that he would rather stay in Manhattan and finish school while living with his father. Even though his school was back east, I was at every teacher conference, school play, graduation, and any other event I thought I should attend.

I was always actively involved in my son's upbringing and education, especially when he was in elementary school. I would fly back to New York every seven to ten days. I was on a first-name basis with the American Airlines flight attendants. They would all tell me to say hi to my son for them.

One of my favorite memories is from when my son was in elementary school, maybe fifth or sixth grade. The Yankees were in the World Series. Tom and I woke up in LA, flew to Oklahoma, Tom argued a case, we got back on our plane, flew to New York, picked up my son, took him to the Bronx, saw the Yankees win, took him back home, kissed him good-bye, told him I'd be back in a week, got on our plane, and came home to fall asleep in our own bed. We did all that in one day.

Whenever we would go to New York, we'd drag my son to every musical in town. Tom and I both love the theater. One Christmas vacation, we went on safari in Africa. We celebrated New Year's Eve by having relay races with my son on the Serengeti Plain. The guide had to drive his truck around the area first to make sure there were no lions around. Later, we hired a tutor and took him out of school for two weeks so he could travel in Europe with us. We'd take this kid everywhere we possibly could. The poor guy has been to more lawyer events than I could wish on anyone.

Tom and my son always had a special bond. Their birthdays are three days apart. Since they're both Geminis, it's like each is the twin the other was promised. When my son was six or seven, we would meet Tom for dinner. Tom drove there separately in his convertible Aston Martin. One time after dinner, I visited the ladies' room, and when I came back, the table was empty. They had decided to play a prank on me by leaving together in Tom's car. I would have been upset if it wasn't so adorable.

Every summer, my son would go to Tom Sawyer Day Camp in Altadena, California. It's right near our house. When that was finished, he would work in the law firm for the rest of the summer. He would carry Tom's briefcase, get coffee, run errands, and sometimes go to court with Tom. That's why he is so comfortable in court as a police officer. He was practically raised there.

When my son was in his probationary year at LAPD, he was stationed downtown. He patrolled the area near Tom's office. One day, something happened on the sidewalk in front of the office. Lynn, the firm's receptionist, is a tough broad from New Jersey. She spotted my son in his uniform handling the incident. She gathered a small crowd of lawyers, pressing their noses against the glass, to watch him in action. They had known him since he was six, and now he was a grown man policing their street.

When we first got married, I was busy being a mother and a wife. But I had other things to do as well. Tom loves to golf, so I decided that I would learn how to play. I started going to the Wilshire Country Club to take lessons with the pro a couple of times a week. I'd also play with my old friend Randy, who worked with me at Chasen's. He and I played on the public course, where we used to get chased by coyotes.

When I figured out that golf is a lot like dancing, I started to get pretty good. It's about precise movement, shifting your body at the right time, and being fluid in your movement. One day, Tom and I were playing at Bel Air Country Club. We both put our balls up on the first tee and hit them out into the fairway. We pulled up to the ball farthest from the hole, the lesser shot. Tom said, "This is yours."

I got out of the cart and looked at the ball. "No, honey," I said. "This is Titleist 2. I'm Titleist 3. This is your ball." I had outdriven Tom on the first hole. That was the last time we ever played golf together. I can't say that I mind. While I loved being out on the beautiful courses and driving the cart, I never had the patience to play a full round the way he does it.

About eight years after moving in to Tom's partially furnished home, we decided it was time to redo the whole house. This would include all the furniture. Tom had been living there since he bought it in the seventies, and it had been redecorated about ten years before I got there. It looked a lot like the steakhouse Houston's, with dark, imposing woods and low lighting.

In the previous remodel, the 1920s-era house had been stripped of all its character. Thank God the interior designer left the important parts like the bronze front door that allegedly came off a Spanish galleon, the bronze central staircase, the travertine floors, and Colombian crotch grain mahogany walls. Upstairs were bedrooms—which would be considered small by modern HGTV standards—for the owners of the house, along with servants' quarters. We redid the upstairs to make the bedrooms larger and added bathrooms. I firmly believe in the saying that the secret to a happy marriage is having separate closets and bathrooms, so those were a must in our house.

When I restored the house, I reintroduced all the great woods, moldings, and Venetian plasters. I imported some really beautiful antique fireplaces and ridiculously gorgeous tiles. I've looked at a lot of fucking houses, and you're going to have to search high and low to beat my finished carpentry. I wasn't fortunate enough to get the original plans for the house, so I couldn't restore it fully to the way the architect intended. I had to go with what I thought was best, keeping with the time period and then adding my own signature to it.

It took about a year and a half to renovate the whole house. While construction was taking place, we moved into our Malibu beach house. Now that it's finished, the house is huge, but it only has three bedrooms: one for me and Tom, one for my son, and one for guests.

That guest room doesn't get used very often, because I don't like to have guests. I've never been the kind of person to invite a lot of people over to my home. We always entertain at a restaurant, a lounge, or somewhere outside of the house. If someone is invited to my home, it's a big deal.

My home is a place where I recharge and escape. It's best when it's calm and serene, and I can enjoy peace and solitude. I didn't grow up with siblings or a big family. I get stressed out if a place is too noisy, even if it's just for a few hours to host a cocktail party. I'd rather do that somewhere else. I know this is all ironic, because the crew of *The Real Housewives of Beverly*

Hills comes to the house all the time. At least this way, people can just see the house on television, and I can still have it quiet most of the time.

For the first decade that I was married to Tom, I worked on projects like that. But let's be honest, I was really well known on Rodeo Drive, too. My closet was full of every kind of dress, shoe, and bauble imaginable. My son was getting older and needing me less. The house was restored and redecorated. I wanted something more. That's when I started to think about performance again.

For a while, I put my career aspirations on hold to tend to Tom. But I needed that time to grow as well. To really come into my own and learn a few things about myself. Only then did I feel ready to get back out there, into the grind of showbiz.

Tom has given me many things. But the sweetest thing he's ever done in my life is believe in me. Renee was my cheerleader and made sure that I got to class. She ensured I had everything I needed growing up. But my husband was the one who really and truly made me feel like I was okay as a human. That I was bright, and my opinions and knowledge mattered. He is the foundation of my strength, confidence, and tenacity.

I watched him for so long. I would watch the way he treats others, the way he leads, and the way he loves his firm and the law. He is very sure of himself. It's like he taught me just by example how to do all those things myself. He made me feel comfortable in my own skin. Now that I was finally comfortable in it, the time had come to shed that skin. To let a whole different version of myself be born. Her name, of course, is Erika Jayne.

10

FANTASY, LOVE, ESCAPE

Erika Jayne is an escape artist. She's not here to cure cancer or create world peace. She's here to offer people a bit of fun. She exists so people who are pressed flesh to flesh on the dance floor can think about her huge blond hair, her conspicuous consumption, and her zero-fucks attitude rather than their own troubles, if only for a minute. But Erika Jayne helped Erika Girardi escape as well.

I married Tom in 2000 and immediately started living his life for the next seven or eight years. I traveled with him, attended his professional events, and watched him get awards. During that time, all I had to worry about was helping Tom and taking care of my boy.

It's easy to lose yourself in the shadow of a powerful man, which I said on *The Real Housewives of Beverly Hills* reunion. It's something I learned from personal experience. There will be plenty of people who say, "Oh, that would never happen to me." If you say that, then you've probably never met a really powerful man.

My feelings about being in Tom's shadow changed when I got a simple piece of mail. It was a postcard featuring a picture of a woman Tom and I both knew. At the time, she was married to one of Tom's colleagues who owns his own firm and does very well for himself. I had heard that she started a singing career and thought, *Oh, that's cool.* This was an invitation to her first concert.

I can still clearly see the image. This woman is a tall, blond European, and in the photo she was wearing a red satin slip dress and standing at a microphone. Her cascade of hair was styled to cover her left eye. It was as if Veronica Lake was doing a cabaret show. The card had her name, the place of the performance, and the date. Then, at the bottom, in small type, it said *Directed by Travis Payne.*

This might not mean a lot to somebody else, but Travis was like a brother to me. We went to Northside High in Atlanta together, and we were in the same performing arts program. We traveled the world as members of the school's tour show, and he starred in the production of *Pippin* that I got suckered into our senior year. Immediately after graduation, Travis was catapulted into the big leagues. He was dancing on tour with Janet Jackson when he was nineteen.

Travis has had an amazing career, choreographing for everyone like Madonna, En Vogue, TLC, Lady Gaga, and all the greats. He has four MTV Video Music Awards for best choreography. He worked extensively with Michael Jackson and was working on the This Is It tour when the King of Pop died. I thought this lady must be taking it seriously if she can afford Travis Payne.

Travis and I had kept in touch after school, and we were friends in LA. I would attend his shows, and he would invite me to his epic house parties. I hadn't talked to him in about a year, but I decided this postcard was a good enough reason to pick up the phone and say hi.

"Hey, I got this invitation at my house," I told him when he answered. "This is fucking crazy!"

"Yeah, it was kind of a cool project," he said.

I was curious how he got involved with this particular woman, because I'd never known him to work for anyone of her level, to be perfectly honest.

"Well, what are you up to? This is all possible for you, too," he said. "Ask anyone."

"Well, if she can do it, I can do it," I said to him, bratty as usual.

"You absolutely should," he said. "Let me show you what's possible. You need to be performing again."

Travis really took me off the bench and saved me. When people are not being their true selves, there's that level of disappointment that turns into anger, resentment, and misery. You see it everywhere in the world, the weight of unrealized dreams. I wasn't going down like that.

Starting the Erika Jayne project was an act of rebellion against everything society told me I should be doing. I should be thankful, pretty, soft, appreciative, quiet, and excited someone rescued me. I had all the things you could have in life when you're thirty-five: a beautiful home, a black AmEx, and a Gulfstream. My kid goes to a great private school with the best tutors and has the best orthodontist. That should be enough. It should be enough to be married to someone who is famous in his career and is influential and changes laws. It should be enough to go to the White House to meet the president. But it wasn't. None of it was enough. I had never realized my own dream.

I looked at those people at the White House and the highbrow functions I would attend with Tom. Then I looked at myself, and I saw no difference. Why not me? Why can't I have success? My husband also gave me a great gift, in that he showed me old ways of thinking are just that. He told me things can happen, but you have to make them happen. I am never afraid to be a hard worker. There is a trick to life, and Tom knows it. When you are with someone as smart and aggressive—and some would say Machiavellian—as he is, it's impossible not to become a student. And *I* am his best fucking protégée.

This is what I was thinking about when Travis set up a meeting with the two of us and Peter Rafelson. Peter is a music producer who helped the woman on the invitation create her project. He also cowrote Madonna's "Open Your Heart," along with dozens of other hit records for Stevie Nicks, Britney Spears, and all sorts of other artists.

At the meeting, Peter explained, "We can create a project. We can create records, and they can be distributed digitally. This is how things work these days."

I kept saying to him, "How is this possible?" I didn't think it actually could be real. I was under no illusions about the music industry. I was a thirty-five-year-old woman. There was no way I was going to walk arms swinging into Capitol Records and walk out with a record contract. They're looking for the next teenager they can mold into a machine that mints money.

What Peter and Travis were offering was something else. I could carve out my own lane, creating my own project, putting it out there ourselves over the internet and directly into the hands of DJs and consumers, and hoping that it caught on. But it was more than that to me. It was a return to a part of myself that I loved but had allowed to languish, which is being a performer. When I created Erika Jayne, it was with no expectations other than reawakening the dragon inside.

I told them that this sounded great, but I'd need to go home and talk to Tom about it. I brought it up that very night. "Tom, I have what I think might be a very interesting opportunity to create again, and I'd really like to do it," I said. "I think that this is a good time for me, and I feel that in my heart. I feel like I need to do this. It's what I know how to do."

Tom being Tom, he wanted to see something on paper. So I went back to Peter, and we put together a document outlining a production budget, including songs, timeline, studio sessions, and everything. I brought that back to Tom so he could see what it looked like.

"This sounds great," he told me. "This is going to be fun." He was a billion percent supportive. You know the reason I believe he was supportive? Because I am one billion percent supportive of him. I've never involved myself in his business. I've never offered unsolicited advice. I've never gotten involved in office politics. I've never done anything other than cheerlead, believe in him, and be present for him. And when the time came for him to be present for me, he was.

The truth is—and I don't think he'd ever admit it now—I don't think he thought we'd be seeing any number one singles on the dance club charts. I don't think he really believed that this was going to lead to everything that it has. Boy, did I show him.

The whole Erika Jayne project was only possible because I'm self-funded. Now, the haters are always going to say, "All you do is spend your husband's money." First of all, it's *our* money. Know how I know? Because the IRS tells us that it is. My name is on that tax return, too.

Second, yes, I have the advantage of a strong checkbook. But I'll tell you what: you can write all the fucking checks you want, but that doesn't guarantee success. That's been proven many times. A record label could write as many checks as it wants, and certain acts aren't getting off the ground. Look at all the checks the losing candidate in an election writes every year. Look at the checks people put into their businesses that don't get off the ground. Does money help everything? Of course. Is it a guarantee of success? No.

Tom gives me two gifts a year: a birthday present and a Christmas present. When this project started, I said to him,

"No Christmas present and no birthday present. My project is my present. That is the gift you can give to me."

He agreed. He kept his word, but every now and then he will say at Christmas, "Well, sweetheart, I can't give you nothing." Now admittedly it is small, but it's still fabulous.

So I started working eight hours a day, four days a week with Peter in the studio. He was always asking me all of these questions: "What do you like? Who inspires you? What are your goals?" He showed me the way to express myself through song and writing music. He was never critical of any of my ideas. Instead he would ask, "Could you flesh that out? What's a better way to say that? How do we translate that into a song?"

I would bring in phrases, poems, and pictures—the things that were inspiring me and were going through my head—and we would make those into song ideas. That's how we created the song "Pretty Mess," which became the name of the album (and the record label, and my Instagram account, and this book, and probably the inscription on my tombstone).

We were writing one day in the studio, and Peter was seated at his keyboard underneath his massive monitors. I was standing next to him, leaning over, and we were both looking at the words on the monitor. We were writing words like "princess" and "temptress" and I said, "Pretty mess."

Peter said, "Hey, wait. What is that?"

"Oh, it's stupid," I said, still a little unsure.

"No. It's actually kind of cool," he said. "Let's keep it."

So we just wrote it down. Then I was thinking about all the different roles you have to play as a woman. Sometimes you're a temptress. Sometimes you're a princess. Sometimes you're a pretty mess. I wrote it out first as a poem: "Everything you see you want. Everything I am I bought." It speaks to the facade of Erika Jayne as a character, something that was still in its infancy when I was thinking about it, but it always had that notion of fantasy, love, and escape.

Those are the three words that really guided her birth: "fantasy, love, escape." I wrote them down one day, and everything that we did had to go back to that mission statement. Later I would add "glitz, glamour, fun." Those six words are the set pieces that support the illusion of Erika Jayne. In every song, every performance, every video, and every costume, it all comes back to those six concepts.

The name Erika Jayne was kind of a mistake. I wanted to just be "Erika," but then it's too close to Madonna or Cher. I hadn't earned one-name status quite yet. Peter finally said, "The only thing that goes with Erika is Jayne."

"Fine, whatever," I said, giving up and hating it a little. Then I read that Joan Crawford hated her stage name because it sounded like "Joan Crawfish," and then I started to equate Jayne with Jayne Mansfield, whom I loved. It started to grow on me.

This period of creation was really special for me, because it was pure expression. There was no corporate executive saying, "This other artist has a hit single, you need to sound like her." There were no expectations. Nobody else knew I was doing this except Tom and Renee. Even if people knew, no one would have cared what the final outcome would have been. No one expected this to go anywhere, so Peter and I could just create exactly what we wanted without any interference.

The first song we recorded was "Give You Everything." Peter was still trying to figure out how well I could sing. "If I sing this, can you sing it back?" he asked.

I was there in the booth with the headphones on, and I opened up my mouth for the first time in a decade. I sang it back to him exactly as he'd sung it to me: "You make me want to give you everything."

"Wow," Peter replied. It was perfect. That was the take that we used on the record. I nailed it. That's how I knew this was the right thing to do, that I was in the right place. Life gives you little signs, and it was something small, but to me it meant everything.

Life said, "Mm-hmm. You're supposed to be here." But then it said, "Okay, now go work for it." Not everything was as easy as that first take. Especially when we started performing again. That's where Travis really came in with the production, the choreography, the costumes, and helping me create the package to support the music.

When we started rehearsing, it was so strange that I really had the jitters. *Why am I so nervous? Why do I feel crazy?* I thought. I'd been dancing and performing since I was a little kid. I felt like it should be second nature to me.

One day, I expressed this to Travis. "You know, Erika, when you step away and try to come back, you get scared," he said. "That's just the way it is. Now get your fucking ass back out there."

I had to get comfortable with feeling uncomfortable. You really have to live and breathe in those moments, because that's where the growth is. The growth isn't when things are good. It's when it's horrible and you stay in it. You improve when you're unsure and it's a struggle. We all have to look stupid and feel like shit in order to evolve.

My goal was to make music and start performing again. A lot of the things I had to go through to get there were painful. But if you cower in those moments of pain, you will never have anything. I thought, *What the fuck are you doing? You've spent this money. You've invested in yourself. You've just got to stick it out.* That's a lot of it. So much of life is sticking it the fuck out.

Finally, we got our first gig. It was at a San Francisco sex party called the Nymphomaniac's Ball at someplace called PleasureZone. It was for straight people, if you can believe it. The DJ had gotten his hands on my music and loved it, and he invited me to come perform three songs. Travis hooked me up with the costume designer Zaldy, a former club kid who has made costumes for Britney Spears, Madonna, Lady Gaga, and worked with Gwen Stefani on her fashion line. He does all of RuPaul's costumes for *RuPaul's Drag Race* and worked with Travis on the costumes for Michael Jackson's This Is It tour. He made me a few rompers—one was fuchsia and one was a pale diamond color—plus an amazing blue catsuit with diamonds on the shoulders. I decided to wear the catsuit for that first night.

I was excited to tell Tom the news. "So we got hired by this sex club. It's kind of like a party they have once every couple of months. I don't know, exactly. But I'm going to go perform."

"Great, hon. Go do it," he said.

"They're going to pay me," I told him.

"Oh, even better," he said. He was excited to see everything I'd been working on and to be there for the first show, so he decided to come with me.

That always surprises people, that Tom would come to a sex party to see me. But let me tell you something: Mr. Girardi does not care. Tom's seen it all, done it all, doesn't care. People think because Tom's older and is a well-respected attorney that he must be prim and proper and a stick-in-the-mud. Nothing could be further from the truth. Nothing fazes Tom. And at the end of the night, he even collected my check from the promoter like he was my business manager.

I showed up at the venue, which was a huge old theater with a gigantic stage. I had four backup dancers and my tracks on a CD, which is funny to think about in the digital age. It had been billed as a sex party, but it wasn't really a scandalous orgy or anything. It was mostly couples and mostly Asian. There was a lot of making out going on, but that was about all I saw. It seemed like the kind of joint couples would go to in order to find a willing third. If Erika Jayne can help set the mood for such assignations, she is absolutely happy to oblige.

I was really hyped to be there, and the DJ was hyped to have us, too. I got out onstage and did our first song, and it was going well. From the stage, I could see the DJ and his setup at the foot of the stage and he was freaking out over the performance. He was dancing and flailing his arms around and just really getting into the whole experience. I finished the first song and started into the second, and the DJ started freaking out again.

I was happy to have the positive feedback, but he got so into dancing that he hit his DJ rig and pulled the whole thing down.

All the wires got pulled out and the lighting board crashed to the floor. Suddenly we were up onstage standing in silence, mortified, while a bunch of confused Asian swingers shot us dirty looks.

I remember standing there thinking, *I should know what to do here.* But I had no clue. It's not like we were going to sing a cappella. What does one do? Someone in the crowd shouted, "Start over!" But you can't just start the show over.

Still stunned, I shouted, "Thank you very much. Have a nice night!" I walked off the stage. The DJ hadn't just exploded his equipment; he also blew up my whole experience.

After that first performance, I thought, *Oh wait a fucking second. That will never happen again.* I made sure that everything was tight for every performance going forward. Not just my dancers, costumes, and singing, but that everything would be technically perfect as well. I wasn't going to let another spastic DJ ruin my show.

Having performed all my life as a young person, I knew the feeling of accomplishment of giving a good show. I didn't get that the first time out. Or even the second time out. It took me awhile to find my groove and get my proficiency back. Even though I wasn't having good shows right away, I knew what the payoff would feel like. So I just had to push through until I got to that other side. I knew that would come from just doing it over and over and over.

I said yes to every show in every dive bar. I've performed on tables, in VIP areas, with no lights, in trains, and on nude beaches. I have performed everywhere. Anywhere someone wanted Erika Jayne to perform, she said yes.

There are two reasons for that. Number one, because I love it. And number two, because I love it.

The audiences weren't always that great. Some people were really into it and knew the project. Some people didn't care. Some people were just assholes. However, there was one thing they couldn't do—they couldn't stop looking. I knew that meant I was on the right track.

Performing wasn't the only way we were getting the word out about Erika Jayne. Peter, Travis, and I went to the Winter Music Conference in Miami a couple of times. It's an event where lots of pop acts and electronic music stars can break out by getting their music into the hands of producers, DJs, remix artists, promoters, and all sorts of people in the industry.

The first single from the *Pretty Mess* album was "Roller Coaster." Strippers used to tell me that they loved to dance to the song, which was the greatest compliment I could ever receive. We decided we should make a music video for the song to try to get it more exposure.

I went to Travis and Peter and told them that I had access to the historic Stardust Casino in Las Vegas. At the time, Tom was on the board of Boyd Gaming, which owned the casino. It was about to be demolished, but there was a window where we could still get inside with a camera crew. Then I told them that Tom and I were going on our annual Christmas trip, which we used to do with about fifty other couples. This year, it would be in the Bahamas and I told them they could come with a small crew.

"I can work with that," Peter said, and he wrote a treatment for the video. The story is something about me having a relationship with a mobster and running away to an island paradise with his employee. I'm abducted to a desert island before escaping once again with my lover, who carries me around shirtless in a pool. It was kind of cliché and all over the place. But what do you want? We were working with what we had.

I was just starting out, and we were making it up as we went along. Travis choreographed it, and you can see him dancing onstage with me at the Stardust along with another dancer. I mean, looking back at it, it's probably kind of dumb. But I had access to this great shit, so why not use it? I was doing what every first timer does: making the most of the resources I had.

It was almost a year between when I started working with

Peter to when "Roller Coaster" was my first number one hit on the dance charts. The day I got the call from Peter is a very special memory for me. I was in Georgia visiting my family for my birthday, which is July 10. I was at my grandmother's house, standing in the driveway. It was, as they say in hell, hot as Georgia in July.

I got a phone call and Peter said, "I just want to let you know that the song is number one on the dance club chart." It would later go on to be the number thirteen song on *Billboard*'s Year End dance club chart for 2007. Not bad for a rookie.

"That's amazing," I told him. I then got to share the news with the rest of my family, including my cousin Jeremy who was standing with me in the driveway when I got the call. He was even more excited than I was. My grandparents were sick at the time, so it was nice that they could be there to share in my success.

Tragically, Jeremy died a few years later when his home burned down. After the fire, Renee and I went by his house. Out on the lawn near the front door were some things that he had tried to save by throwing them out of the front door as it burned. Among those things was a copy of my first CD.

At the funeral, I told my uncle that I had seen it there on the lawn. "He was playing it all the time," my uncle said enthusiastically. "I had to tell him, 'You need to give poor Erika a rest!'"

It's nice to have that memory with Jeremy in the driveway. It was a special moment. It means a lot that he enjoyed my music and was proud of me.

In that year, I had overcome a lot of obstacles and got back to one of the things that I loved the most. And when I had my first number one single, I proved a lot of people wrong. There were plenty of people who didn't think I could do it.

"Well, you know, it's a really tough business and you're way too old," people would say condescendingly at cocktail parties when they heard about my new venture. They thought I was starting from scratch. They thought I was just some bored housewife who woke up at thirty-five and thought she was going to start singing and dancing. But no, motherfucker, that's not it. They had no idea that I was trained, I had lived this life before, and I had not only the skill but also the determination to make it work.

The internet also made all this possible. Being able to digitally distribute our music ripped the cover off the industry, and all the old rules were out the window. That made it possible for an "ancient" artist like me to find a foothold and be discovered, appreciated by fans, and able to sell records.

It was so great to have people ask, "Oh, how's your little singing and dancing thing coming along?"

I would say, "Oh, it's good. It's good." I didn't need to enumerate my successes or tell them I'm *Billboard*'s number forty-two dance track artist of all time to prove them wrong. I knew I had accomplished what I set out to do. And I wasn't lying. It was going well.

When I listen to *Pretty Mess* now, there are still some great songs on there, but not all of it is amazing. It sounds like a beginning. You can point back to any singer's first album, any director's first film, or any author's first book and see the mistakes they made. But you can also see what is great about them. That album is like a fawn standing up on four legs and learning to walk. It's a little wobbly, but it gets there. You can hear the creation—right or wrong, good or bad—of *something*.

I like to say that without Erika Jayne, Erika Girardi would just be another rich bitch with a plane. That is true. After all of those years of living Tom's life, there was nothing more I could buy. There were no clothes collections, no garages full of cars, no amount of anything that was going to bring me the level of satisfaction that I have today. Without my project, I would have been relegated to a life of shopping, sitting on a few charity boards of no consequence, and standing silently by my husband's side full of unrealized potential. That was what I was expected to do. Instead, I do what I love. I create.

Even more than anyone else needed Erika Jayne to escape, I did.

11

GLITZ, GLAMOUR, FUN

y first live performance with my creative director, Mikey Minden, was at Los Angeles Pride
in 2009. This is a huge, weekend-long gay pride concert that
attracts such major acts that *LA Weekly* calls it "gay Coachella."
It culminates in a giant concert on Sunday night when all of
West Hollywood comes out to party.

That year, we were performing on the smaller stage where
the lesser-known acts appear during the day as all the Ls, Gs,
Bs, Ts, and Qs enjoyed themselves under the rainbow flags in
the hot June sun. I hired Mikey, a skilled choreographer, to
up Erika Jayne's performance game, and that's what he did for
Pride. He put me on stage with four male dancers and had us
work every inch of ourselves for the crowd.

I was wearing a gray, black, and silver Brian Lichtenberg catsuit with a middle corset and, of course, a pair of knee-high Chanel boots. All of a sudden, in the middle of the set, I rolled my ankle, almost like it collapsed on itself. It was a combination of me getting a little too enthusiastic in my performance ("over-living," Mikey would say) and the stage being slippery.

This wasn't the first time it had happened to me, and it happens to every performer at times during her career (yes, even Beyoncé). There I was, crouched down for a moment and a bit stunned, and I looked up at Mikey who was standing in the wings of the stage.

He looked straight into my eyes and shook his head from right to left as if to say, "Bitch, do not give up. If you give up right now, you're dead."

I will never forget that one little movement, because that was just what I needed. Someone to remind me that the key to being a great performer is rolling with whatever happens, thinking on your feet, and being comfortable with being uncomfortable. My dancer Sean Braithwaite bent down and picked me up, and I continued like nothing had happened. Let me tell you, this was no little sprain. It got quite painful, but I never let the crowd know there was anything wrong.

With that little bit of pushy encouragement, Mikey and I forged a bond that can't be broken.

I had first met Mikey while I was still promoting singles from the *Pretty Mess* album, and I felt like Erika Jayne needed a change. You know when artists become stale? It's when they stop challenging themselves and become complacent. You have to keep the collaborative vein open. Once you close that down, once you're not willing to look outside and say wow, that's a new, fresh take on something, that's when you become uninspired and not fresh. Trust me, I'm always fresh, and we're always bringing in young talent to reinvigorate the act.

I was introduced to Mikey through the late Jerry Heller, the manager who was behind the rap group NWA. Tom had once provided Jerry and NWA rapper Easy E with some legal advice. Jerry's nephew was doing some road managing for me and said, "You know who you need to meet? This kid Mikey Minden. He's amazing."

At the time, Mikey was the creative director for the Pussycat Dolls show in Las Vegas. He really helped Pussycat Dolls creator Robin Antin take her creation to the next level. What he was doing there was very much in line with the hair-whipping, floor-working insanity that is Erika Jayne. He was only twenty-four years old when we met at a restaurant. He walked in, bold and confident, in full Mikey regalia, with arms full of bracelets, fingers full of rings and his then-signature perfectly waxed eyebrows. Before he even sat down, he said to me, "Have we met before?"

I don't think we ever had, but it was almost like we did. He's one of those people I just hit it off with on so many levels. A month later, after we shot the "Give You Everything" video, I was at his twenty-fifth birthday party at Apple Lounge in West Hollywood. We have been friends and collaborators ever since.

He perfectly understood Erika Jayne and what I was trying to do with her. Both Travis and Peter had worked with the greats of the music industry and lent a certain amount of polish to our work together. They thought Erika Jayne should be a perfect, sparkling diamond. Immediately Mikey brought his grit and youthful defiance to the project. It was like he was saying, "Oh, you think you're fancy, Erika? Let me show you what I think."

Mikey reexamined everything I'd done so far. Everything with Peter and Travis was technical, but with Mikey it was raw and rule breaking. He saw something different, and we were able to expand on it and keep going, which is really cool.

I was reaching into my gut and figuring out what this project was, who I wanted to embody, and what I wanted to say. There's a theme to the whole Erika Jayne experience, which is ripping off the layers of myself to get to the person inside. It's about being comfortable enough to reveal the darker, sexier, secret side that polite society frowns upon that all of us have lurking in our subconscious and that's dying to get out.

The best thing about our working relationship is that we really push each other. If I wanted to push any limit—or what I felt was pushing a limit—Mikey would say to me, "Bullshit. You should go further, and let me tell you why." He encouraged me to really be free, be fearless, and embrace this entire over-the-top, provocative doll character that we created.

The first thing we worked on together was the music video for "Give You Everything," which was the first track we recorded for *Pretty Mess* but the third single I released. I already had a director and a concept for the video. Basically it's a little story about me falling in love with a guy who is trying out to be one of my dancers. There were a bunch of dance breaks, and Mikey came in to choreograph those.

I already had the hair and makeup in place, but Mikey suggested a team of stylists as well. Just like me, he thinks wardrobe is where the character really comes out. Those costumes lent an edgier and fresher vibe, for sure. We went up to film the video at a public elementary school in Santa Barbara. They had the most beautiful theater I'd ever seen in my life. It was Spanish Mission–style that had been completely restored and was full of top-of-the-line equipment. It was absolutely stunning.

The next video was going to be for the song "Pretty Mess." I had such a great time with Mikey on "Give You Everything" that I gave him even more control over this video. He codirected it with the photographer, Mike Ruiz, but now he was truly taking on the role of creative director as well as doing the choreography. With this video, Mikey and I were able to make the vision tighter and more our own. We wanted to focus more on the performance, fashions, and lifestyle. We wanted to build up that persona.

The point of these videos—or any videos really—is that I needed to make pictures for the people. If I'm going to say "pretty mess," we need to show what that looks and feels like. Mikey and I always say, "You can only wear so many costumes." The message I'm trying to convey is in these pictures, in the subtlety. It's about defining myself visually as an artist and creating my signature. It's about putting on the outside the things that only I have in the interior.

That is still one of my favorite videos, and you can see Mikey's fingerprints all over it. The hair is bigger, the dancing is edgier, the costumes are skimpier, and I'm just pushing everything right to the edge. We even did our own homage to Busby Berkeley by filming me on a bed from above, surrounded by my backup dancers. I don't think Busby ever would have put me in a sparkly onesie with garters, though.

That video also costars Johnny and Anthony, my two male dancers who pranced around in high heels and sported a very androgynous look. By now, everyone has seen boys dancing in high heels in music videos by Madonna and Lady Gaga, but Mikey likes to claim that we did it first. I'm not entirely sure it's true, but we certainly were *among* the first.

Johnny and Anthony are both excellent dancers, and they became two of my closest friends. They're both incredibly technical. We would rehearse just the three of us, and I would match their movements. They would lovingly correct me, and they encouraged me to step out and be comfortable with a totally different style of movement. They made me a much better dancer and performer. They're both also absolutely insane lunatics with hearts of gold, which makes for a really fun time when we tour together.

Ever since the shoot for "Pretty Mess," whenever we want to make a new video, Mikey and I do almost everything ourselves. We hire a producer and a director of photography to shoot it, but we're in charge of all the other creative aspects of the shoot. I think that's what is really powerful about the videos. Say what you want, but I do have some killer videos—and it comes down to the same two people driving the vision.

Eventually, it came time to retool my live show, which is how we ended up at that fateful LA Pride performance in which Mikey dragged me up from the ground just using his eyes from the side of the stage. (He still stands there now, dance-moming during every performance and giving me the thumbs-up when it's going well.)

What Mikey brought to the show is what we call "the full fantasy." It's the mane of hair, edgy makeup, provocative costumes, backup dancers, props, lighting, and all the decadence you see on stage with Erika Jayne that you won't see many other places. It's also the little wink that we know this is all a bit wonderfully absurd. It's meant to be a sensory overload, just knocking the audience over the head with our vision. It's like a hurricane hitting the crowd all at once and hopefully sweeping them off of their feet.

One of Mikey's skills is that he has a way of making even the smallest performance in the tiniest space seem important. He finds a way to do the most with what we have and makes the show a million times better than it should be, given a venue's limitations—and almost every venue has its limitations.

After we released all the singles from the first album, I was thinking about recording some more music. In my opinion, if you're sitting on your ass not thinking about the next project, you're never going to grow, and you're essentially dead.

That process of creating new music is interesting, because the real superstars are hard to get and very expensive. The marketplace is flooded with "producers" and "songwriters" who are basically bullshit. Finding good people to work with is really about making enough noise and getting well enough known that people will want to collaborate.

The hard part for me has always been finding people who know what I'm about. It's not like I'm a pop act or a girl group, where they can write a cute song about chasing boys, partying all night long, or heartache. It's different when you have a grown woman with life experience under her belt (or corset).

Also, I'm not an artist with a development deal at a major label. I don't have some musical godfather who magically drops me in the lap of a multiplatinum Grammy-winning producer. I also don't have the corporate financial backing. That is hard to beat sometimes.

Instead of doing things the old way, I develop relationships with people I like and who make music I like. It's about listening to a lot of music and reaching out and asking if people want to work together. Sometimes I get a quick yes, and sometimes it's an even quicker no. Sometimes I'll hear: "I charge $1 million a song," which is just a passive-aggressive way of saying no. It's crazy when people quote these outrageous fees, as if anyone is worth that kind of dough these days, when only about five people make real money in this industry.

While Mikey and I collaborate on my look, costumes, videos, and performances, he's never been involved in the production or writing of the music. Of course I will play him tracks and ask for his opinions about things, but when it comes to making the songs, that's on me.

After *Pretty Mess* came and went, I started working with this music industry veteran to try to take the project to a larger audience. He had the pedigree, had worked with some really major people in the industry, and had written some huge hits. On paper, it all made sense.

Working with him, however, was a disaster. Almost like a born-again Christian, he always raised an eyebrow at my persona. I feel like he was in it for all the wrong reasons, which was to take the money rather than to further my project. He also wasn't really looking for any input from me at all.

This person had had a successful career in the age of the big record business. But I felt he wasn't familiar enough with the ways things were changing in the industry. The music was decent. It was very well-made pop. I never sang higher, and I never sang harder. But I wasn't totally in control, and I didn't like that. When I would suggest things, he'd respond with, "Yeah, but we're doing it this way. Just wait and see what happens."

That was always the wrong answer, because to me it meant that he had not paid any attention to how I got here, who I was, and what I was really trying to say. He had a very narrow view of what success looks like, which is just so far from who I am and from the project that I had created. I felt like it was taking me from something edgy and cool to something that was much more dull and conventional.

He was coming from what I call a "me too" place. You know the artists who hear the hottest new sound or the cool new producer and they say, "Oh, me too, me too," even if that sound or that producer has absolutely nothing to do with the message they're trying to convey? It's more of a grab for attention and popularity than it is about creating something that is original to that artist. It almost always fails. No artist should ever be caught up in chasing every musical trend—they should be setting them.

For instance, we made a track called "Get It Tonight" with Flo Rida, who is a supersweet guy and a great artist. At the time, he was killing every chart imaginable, so it totally made sense to have him be the featured artist on my song. It's a cute little track, but not exactly Erika Jayne's sensibility. For the first time, I felt like I was trying to be too young. Not only did it feel like a stretch, it was also inauthentic.

It's a great pop track, don't get me wrong, but it doesn't have any of my signature or personality. Any other artist could have sung it, and it would have been just the same. The sound was very much what was happening at the time and middle of the road, but nothing at all specific to Erika Jayne.

This time I made the video with a new team, and Mikey wasn't involved. He and I were talking during this whole process, so Mikey knew what I was working on. There were no hard feelings, but I sure did miss him on set.

Looking at the video now, it just isn't Erika Jayne, either. It looks like a commercial for some South American soft drink you've never heard of. Everything is bright colors and bubblegum sensibility. It's like they sanded all of the grit off of Erika Jayne, but we weren't left with a unique jewel—just something in the middle, nothing special and not cool at all.

Let me tell you something: there is a way to make anything cool. There is a way to change things, even if it's subtly, so you could make a Cracker Barrel look like Studio 54. But what you can't do is all of a sudden turn an artist into someone they're not. That's what these people were trying to do to me.

I didn't promote the track at all. None of this is to blame Flo Rida, who was just a featured artist and did his job. I can't imagine what the track would have been like without him. It was the team around me that wasn't carrying their weight. The producer I was working with did some mediocre remixes that I didn't have my hand in. That is why I don't really talk about that record today. I never felt involved. It got to a place where I had to finish out this project, and I didn't really like who these people were.

There is a whole album worth of material that I never

released, because I wasn't happy with it. It wasn't going to do anything for the Erika Jayne project. That whole experience cost me dearly in multiple ways, and it taught me a lot.

Once I finally cut ties with the team, I called up Mikey and said, "Listen, I'm finally free of these fools, let's get back to doing what we do."

"I've been waiting, bitch," he said.

Shortly after that I was introduced to Charles Koppelman, the former CEO of EMI music. Charles was working as a brand consultant for me and introduced me to producers like Scott Storch, Aaron Pearce, and Chris Rodriguez. That's when I started making things I liked again. I worked a lot in Miami, where Scott produced "Crazy." Chris helped me take "Painkillr," which I had written as a poem a year before, and lay down the beats to make it into a song. It's about how losing yourself in love can be a bit like losing yourself in drugs. Both can be numbing experiences, as destructive as they are intoxicating.

Aaron also introduced me to Justin Tranter, one of the greatest songwriters I've had the chance to work with (and certainly the funniest). Justin was the front man of the band Semi Precious Weapons and had just opened for Lady Gaga on her tour. We made about six tracks together, and I later got to work with Justin again when we wrote "How Many Fucks."

The great thing about Justin is that he is really able to crawl into an artist's brain and pull out all of the best thoughts and whip them into something absolutely brilliant. He's written songs for Justin Bieber, Kelly Clarkson, Britney Spears, and all sorts of other top acts, and I've just loved watching his career explode. He was recently nominated for his first Grammy, and I couldn't be happier for him! No one deserves success more than he does. You do get to meet some really great people along the way, and Justin and Aaron are two of them.

Steven Johnson was the one good thing I took away from my miserable experience with that producer. Steven produced the "Get It Tonight" video, and he's just magnificent. I got him on board to produce the video for my song "Crazy" as well.

We wanted the video to look like a downtown LA warehouse party. Everyone from every different walk of life, socioeconomic group, race, ethnicity, and sexual orientation all came out to have one giant banger. The set was just like the incredible party it was trying to depict, except we filmed it in the middle of August, and it was hot and sticky the whole time.

But it was so much fun, and the video looks amazing. It's like a clash between biker gang culture, stripper culture, tattoo culture, and rave culture, with a hot guy wearing a gorilla mask thrown in for good measure. I was back to that gritty feel that I had been missing.

Then I decided to make a video for "Painkillr," which Mikey

and I produced and directed ourselves. The day we made that video was magical.

We did something somewhat unusual, which was staging the photo shoot right before we shot the video. If you ask anybody in their right fucking mind, they would say it's almost impossible to do them both in one day and do them right. But that's just a testament to how organized Mikey and I are.

I needed new press photos. Joe Labisi, who was the director of photography on "Crazy" and "Painkillr," is also a still photographer. I asked him to do them before we shot the "Painkillr" video. I didn't have the same hair, makeup, or costumes as I did in the video, so that added many more setups to an already ambitious day.

I went from the photo shoot to a setup in a bed, to a setup in a cage with two other dancers, to dancing on concrete. It was a hell of a workday at Siren Studios in Hollywood, but it was one of my favorite days ever. The reason why is because everyone on the team was doing *them*. Mikey and I told them the essence of what we wanted the shoot to be and supplied a folder full of images for references. Everyone—hair, makeup, wardrobe, lighting, photography—came back and said, "What do you think of this?" and every choice was perfect. Everyone brought their specific vision to the video, and they all melded into something phenomenal and singular.

It turned out exactly the way we wanted it to be: raw, in your face, aggressive, sexy, and all in black and white. For a song called "Painkillr," this was exactly the treatment it needed. It was like stripping Erika Jayne down to the bare essentials and letting her be entirely uninhibited.

The first live show we did after that was in Dallas. It was the birth of the black-compression-catsuit moment of my career. For that performance it was just simple and one color, but then we started upping our game with rhinestones, jewels, and all the other glitz, glamour, and fun.

In Dallas we had four boys and two girls, new costumes, new songs, and it was just perfect. It was the end of summer, so it was a warm night. I left everything on the stage that night. I had the biggest smile on my face, because my team and I were back together.

After that, I did one song, "You Make Me Want to Dance," cowritten by Ross Vallory of Journey and remixed by an Asian producer. I dragged Mikey and the glam squad to the Philippines to shoot the video. This is another one of Erika Jayne's adventures. I'm always showing up and saying to the team, "Guys, we have an opportunity to make a video in Manila," or, "Guys, we have an opportunity to go perform on an aircraft carrier in the Persian Gulf."

The response I always get is, "What?" But then we find a way of pulling it off, and it's always a fantastic experience.

We filmed the video in Manila in the middle of the summer on the hottest day of the year, which wasn't the best idea. We were filming street scenes in which I'm backed up by the dance crew G Force, which is huge over there. But it was so hot that we had to film in the middle of the night so it would be cooler. Still, I thought I was going to pass out under all of my hair and makeup.

The part of town we were filming in was pretty rough, too. There were stray cats and rats everywhere, and we had to make sure they weren't ruining any of our shots. But we got all the material we needed. The crew and I did a big production number in the streets, with me sitting on top of a tuk-tuk with ERIKA JAYNE emblazoned on it in big yellow letters.

A few months later, after the single came out, I took four female dancers and Mikey through a sweep of Asia. We hit Seoul, Tokyo, Manila, and Singapore over the course of two weeks. It was my first time in Seoul and Singapore, so I had no idea what to expect.

We were supporting the single and had four great shows and a wonderful response. Our final performance in Singapore was at a club called 1-Altitude, which is the world's highest outside bar. It was a warm night and we were all standing around a table celebrating our successful run and our return home the next day.

Mikey had a few shots, and he was showing the girls how they should have been doing the head roll during one of the numbers in the show. He started swirling his head around and around in a circle, and then he whacked his forehead on top of the Grey Goose bottle sitting on the table. It had one of those metal quick-pour nozzles on top, and that cut Mikey's forehead. He hit that bottle so hard that he sheared the top right off of it.

I looked at him and said, "Are you okay? Do you need to go to the hospital?" His cut was bleeding a lot, like a wound to the face always will, so it looked pretty bad.

"No, I'm okay," he told me.

"Well, then let's keep going," I said. That's how we do things in my crew. Unless you have to be hospitalized, nothing is going to stop the party. Mikey didn't need stitches but he did have a giant knot the next morning. He might have been feeling no pain the night before, but it caught up with him on the ride home.

I can't begrudge Mikey for wanting to blow off some steam. There is pressure on me, but there is pressure on him, too. Sometimes I forget how much of the weight he shoulders for me. I'm out front, but he is the one who keeps the girls in line, deals with technical issues, and makes sure it all works the way it's supposed to.

The minute I left behind that old-school producer and returned to my people, I started to get my momentum going. We went from "Painkillr" and "Crazy" right into "How Many Fucks" and eventually "XXPEN$IVE." I knew that Erika Jayne had found her stride. I wasn't looking back, I was running forward.

I always feel like the clock is ticking, especially in this profession. Everything has to be a run for the end zone. Erika Jayne didn't arrive on the scene until many women are leaving the music business. I'm not only making up for lost time, but I'm doing it on borrowed time.

Mikey and I talk every day on the phone at 7:30 a.m. while we watch *Good Morning America*. We start talking about Mikey's personal life, then about my personal life, and then about twenty minutes later, we finally get to talk about an upcoming show or a costume fitting or photo shoot. Sometimes he just calls me at 7:30 to tell me he's on his way over and he'll be there in fifteen minutes so we can do all of this in person.

Beyond work, Mikey is someone I really love and cherish my friendship with. It's like we're of one mind now. Mikey is my closest confidant. I admit my anxieties, fears, frustrations, and self-loathing to him. He knows my husband, my son, and my mom. He's at my house so often people think he lives in my closet. You can't travel the world and spend that much time with someone and not know them through and through.

It's not as if we never have our differences. When he knows he is about to say something I might not like, he'll lead with, "Just hear me out before you say something. What we have done before is this . . ." Usually that ends with me finishing his sentences. We're always thinking the same thing at the same time, like we have some sort of crazy psychic bond.

In June 2017, I was back performing at LA Pride, but this time I was headlining on the main stage. We were at the hot, dusty sound check early in the day, and I was feeling overwhelmed by everything. Especially because this was the first time that I'd be performing since I hurt my shoulder on *Dancing with the Stars*. I was also bringing back my high-heeled dancers Johnny and Anthony for the occasion, so I was a little emotional.

"You know, I'm a little freaked out about coming back to LA Pride," I told Mikey, because last time had been such a disaster.

"Yeah, but you're so much different, Erika," he said.

"Do you remember the first Pride we did on that tiny little stage up the street?" I asked.

"Oh, do I!" he said.

"I'll never forget the way you shook your head when I fell," I said. I looked at him and I knew it wouldn't happen again.

We killed that performance. They wanted boys, I gave them boys. They wanted hot sluts, I gave them hot sluts. I even threw in some nineties reminiscences, giant LED screen graphics, pyrotechnics, and glitter cannons. It was the Super Bowl halftime show of West Hollywood. As always, I gave the gays everything they wanted.

I thanked the crowd and walked offstage. Mikey was dance-moming right where he should be, at the side of the stage. He was jumping up and down, and we both just started screaming. We were so excited, not just for this performance, but for all of them. For all of the crappy ones that didn't go as planned, for all of that time we weren't together and I was working with fools, for just how far we'd taken this whole thing.

I knew I'd put on a good show and that people liked it. I knew what we had set out to do and that everything had gone exactly as we had planned. The show went off without a hitch, and the crowd went home happy. I felt my own sense of pride that we had come from that little stage down the street all the way to the main stage to close the show. It was also nice that they chose *me* as the headliner, even though they could have selected one of the bigger acts that went on before me. Everything had come full circle in such a satisfying way, it was like the ending of a movie.

The silly credit sequence of this movie would have been shot later in my suite at the London Hotel, where Mikey and I got well lit on more than a couple of celebratory cocktails. But hey, I think we really earned them!

12

REBORN ON THE FOURTH OF JULY

rika Jayne was built and perfected at Pride performances, gay clubs, and circuit parties, which are
high-production, all-night sweaty gay dance parties with thousands of shirtless boys (and probably a psychoactive drug or
two). I've always been lucky to have a huge gay following. As
Saturday Night Live joked, I'm the Kitty Ambassador to the
Twink Republic of Qwonk. One reason is I make dance music,
and no one likes dance music like gay guys.

There's a deeper connection between Erika Jayne and the
gay community, though. I think the character has always been
about having the audacity to be herself, and not give a fuck
what anyone says. She is always comfortable in her own skin

and says, "This is my life. This is who I am. I embrace myself, and I embrace those around me." I think that gay people, more than anyone else, understand how important that is. There is a lot to gain by living out loud and being proud—even for this straight woman.

A couple of years into my project, I hooked up with Orlando Puerta, who owns Citrusonic, a company that does music marketing and live events. He books a lot of acts for pride events all around the country and was instrumental in getting me in front of a gay audience.

Back when this project was just starting, I would do a gig anywhere, no matter if people were paying attention or not. I literally danced on a tiny card table in a VIP section of a Miami club to get my music more attention. I also love performing, so to me even the world's smallest stage is better than no stage at all.

I performed more than once at Splash, the legendary gay club in Manhattan. They used the stage for go-go boys to take showers in their bathing suits over the dance floor (which is why they called it Splash). So my dancers and I would be on that stage trying not to slip or get our feet stuck in the drains on the tiled floor. As a side note, my son went to high school down the street from Splash. They had open campus for lunch, so they could walk around the neighborhood and go wherever they wanted. One time there was a poster of me in the window of the club advertising an upcoming performance, and my son saw it walking back from school. He was too embarrassed to tell his friends, but he called to tell me about it. His tone implied, "Really, Mom?"

At a recent show in Vegas, after my second song finished, the lights and sound mysteriously shut off. Not just onstage, but in the whole club. I looked from right to left and thought, *Where's the next musical cue?* I said, "Thank you," to the cheering crowd, so I knew the microphone worked. When I saw that it was panic city in the sound booth, I quickly realized the music would be returning as soon as it was fixed. I immediately popped up and said to the crowd, "I thought I'd take this time to say how much I really appreciate you all supporting me," and blah-blah-blah. I was making things up to kill time.

Through the darkness, I could barely see Mikey on the other side of this big room, looking at me like, "Just keep talking." I saw my soundman working the shit out. All of a sudden—boom!—the lights are back on and the music cue hits. It was impressive that the show was falling apart and the crowd thought the whole thing was planned. I wish we were that genius.

Sometimes, especially in those early years, the audience

would be really into me, and other times they wouldn't. Still, Mikey choreographed every show like it was a performance at the MTV Video Music Awards. I performed like it was, too, no matter how many yawns we got from the guys at Splash wishing I were a go-go boy instead.

Even that rejection, though, made me a better performer. You have to be willing to be ridiculed, laughed at, and mocked. You have to have people not believing in you. That makes you your own biggest cheerleader. That makes you say, "This is do or die, and there is no way I'm going to fail up here."

Forgetting that motto is the real failure. Fuck it if your costume falls apart or you twist your ankle or the DJ knocks the soundboard over. Shit happens. It's when the performer doesn't bring it, that's where the failure is. I've failed many times when I was afraid or not feeling it or being bratty. That's not what the people pay for. I always need to remind myself of this truth.

That said, there have been a lot of crazy Erika Jayne shows over the years. One year, we played a Toronto Pride event on Hanlan's Point Beach. It's a popular nude beach with a huge gay following. (I learned from a plaque near the venue that it is where Babe Ruth hit his first home run, which is bizarre.)

We did our sound check early in the morning and everything seemed cool. But by the afternoon when we got onstage, half of the people in the crowd were just totally naked. I'm used to Erika Jayne being the person in the club wearing the least amount of clothing, but not this time. I looked down at that crowd and thought, *Wow, you people have nerve. I thought I had nerve, but I'm a damn fool. So, good for you.*

No matter what I did, or what happened on that stage, nobody could call me crazy that day. I was working with my two androgynous dancers, Johnny and Anthony, plus four other male dancers wearing next to nothing. But why would anyone want to look at them when there was full nudity everywhere around us? All the guys on that stage with me had performed with Britney Spears or Christina Aguilera or some other diva. They thought they'd seen it all, but it took Erika Jayne to deliver their first performance for a nude *audience.*

One of my worst gigs of all time was in San Francisco. We were set to perform at a winter-themed circuit party. We went and did the sound check and the venue was all tricked out in a really cute way. The stage even had this huge polar bear on it.

We came back to the club that night and were all dressed in costume and ready to go. The security guy was at the back door and said, "They look young," pointing to my four male dancers. He asked them for their IDs but they didn't have them. They were in costume and we were never told we would need IDs.

I told him that they're all over twenty-one and we just don't have our IDs on us. Then another guy (who I later found out was an off-duty San Francisco police officer hired by the club) stepped in. "Yeah, I need to see their IDs," he said.

"We've been hired to perform," I explained. "We're just going to do our show and leave. We're not going to hang out."

He pulled me aside and was being kind of a dick to me, talking at me rather than listening to me. Finally he said, "Ma'am, I'm a police officer," as if to explain he wasn't just some bouncer, as if his authority could somehow intimidate me.

"My son's a police officer," I replied. "So what? What does that have to do with this?"

He questioned the boys, and obviously they all told the truth about being of legal age. Finally, he let us inside. We went upstairs and were waiting in the greenroom. All of a sudden this police officer, the same guy, came up to me and said, "You gotta leave."

"Why?" I said, not in a loud voice. It's funny, when I get challenged on a level like that, I don't become rude, but just very matter-of-fact. I'm certainly not intimidated. I was angry more than anything, because this felt personal. We were there to do a job and this aggressive off-duty police officer was interrupting our whole show.

He said to me, "It's because you said something to someone and they want you to leave. So let's go."

"I didn't say anything to anybody. We just came up here and started getting ready. Who told you that?" I said.

"I told you to leave," he said, getting in my face a little.

"I didn't talk to anyone," I said, still not raising my voice. I was being very defiant at this point, because I don't like to be bullied. It was bullshit. To me, this cop should have been worried about the obviously intoxicated people in the crowd. They were breaking more rules than we were that night. I don't know why his focus was on us and not these other people who, in my opinion, looked underage and like they were about to pass out.

"You're going to have to leave," he said again. "Now."

I stared at him, and I just went, "Okay." I shook my head, as if to say, "Whatever, dick."

I took the slowest, most defiant walk out of that club. I mean, it was so slow, so calm. They threw us all out before we even got a chance to perform.

But they would not let my soundman, John, back in to get our tens of thousands of dollars of sound equipment. We had set it up during sound check. We all went back to the hotel and John stayed there and waited until the party was over, at which point they finally just threw it all out on the street. He put it back in the SUV and finally got to come home. Ever since then, we have a rule: everyone brings their ID to every performance—no matter how old they look or how few pockets their costumes have.

Not all promoters are as unprofessional as that one in San Francisco. I've worked with Jeffrey Sanker, who throws the White Party in Palm Springs every Easter Weekend. In 2016, I was named Queen of White Party and invited to headline the main stage. This weekend-long gay dance event attracts thirty thousand people, and Jeffrey always has his act together. His production is totally top notch. We gave them the full fantasy, as Mikey and I like to call it, serving up killer costumes, a dozen dancers, glitter bombs, pyrotechnics, and my giant LED screen projections.

I was so impressed by Jeffrey's stage. When we walk into a venue, we have no idea what we're going to get. Madonna—who brings her own stage on every stop of a tour—and Britney Spears—who is performing on the same stage every night in Las Vegas—have the luxury of knowing the exact topography they're performing on. They know where the dips and creases are, where the elevators come up, and what the slope of the stage is.

When you're me, sometimes you're on fucked-up stages that are cobbled together on an uneven surface. There might be holes in the stage, or there are weird dips in it, or you have to make sure not to trip on the floor drain, like at Splash. One of the first things I have to do as a performer is go out and look, so I know what I'm working with. At this point in my career, I can walk into any venue and immediately assess its strengths and weaknesses. Then I tailor my show to maximize it within its limitations.

That's what I need to do so I can go out there and not think about anything other than performing. So I can deliver what the people came to see. Peace of mind is something every performer really needs, no matter if we're at the biggest concert venue on the planet or some rickety card table in a VIP room.

Another memorable show took me halfway across the world. One day, Tom came home and said, "You're gonna go do this thing for this lawyer guy I know and perform on one of those, I don't know, one of those ships."

"What are you talking about?" I asked him.

"Yeah, I committed you. He'll call you."

See, the thing about Tom is that everything is really casual with him. He'll say, "Meet me for dinner tonight," and then you show up and it's like a black-tie gala.

Eventually, this lawyer I've never met before called me. He said he asked Tom if I would be interested in performing and Tom told him I'd love to. "We're so excited to have you," he said. "Here's what you need to do to get all of your security clearances."

Excuse me? Security clearances? I said, "Sir, could you please tell me exactly what this gig is?"

He told me he was with a civilian organization called Cooks from the Valley, based in Bakersfield, California. Every year, they go to different ships and aircraft carriers all over the world and throw July Fourth barbecues for service members. I was being enlisted to perform at one of these barbecues.

When Tom got home that night, I was a little miffed that he had signed me up for such an event without asking me first. "I'm not even sure I want to do this," I said.

"You're doing this because it's going to be an interesting experience," he told me. "Trust me."

Now I had to sell this to my team. I went to Mikey and said, "Well, the boss said that we have to go do this performance on a ship for a bunch of sailors for July Fourth. He said it's going to be interesting."

"Sailors on a ship?" Mikey asked. "Well, I guess we're going to need some female dancers."

I was forty-one and I had just gotten a nose job at the beginning of June. It had only been a few weeks since I'd had the surgery. You're not even supposed to wear heavy sunglasses, much less whip your head around, so soon after getting the procedure. I still had two black eyes.

We were booked to do a morning show in Toronto. I took four female dancers, my hair and makeup guys Preston and Michael, my sound guy, and my assistant at the time to go do it. Then we were leaving right from there to go perform on the USS *Enterprise*. No, not the one with Captain Kirk. It's the aircraft carrier where they filmed *Top Gun*. At that time it was deployed in the Persian Gulf.

We flew to Maine, where the military transport would pick us up. We got on the plane with the Cooks from the Valley crew and all the meat they were going to be grilling for the troops. "So, Erika Jayne is going in with the steaks," we overheard someone say to a commanding officer.

My dancer Erin leaned over to me and said, "We should forever be known as Erika Jayne and the Steaks." It's something I still laugh about to this day.

We flew from Maine to Shannon in Ireland, then to Crete, and then to Bahrain. This was a military transport, so far from business class it made me yearn for economy. Even to get up and go to the bathroom was an ordeal. We were just trying to endure all of these flights and get some sleep when we could, because when we got to our destination we'd have to perform.

After the long journey, we checked into the Diplomat Radisson Blu Hotel in Bahrain, which was fabulous. It's where the former vice president Joe Biden stayed when he was there. After all of those rough flights, my face was just throbbing. To make it worse, the dust in the desert gave me an ear, nose, and throat infection.

The next day, we performed in the theater at the base in Bahrain. It was great. We did meet and greets afterward, and this one soldier came up and said, "I have to tell you my wife's been a big fan of yours for a long time because she loves club music. Can we take a picture?" Of course I was happy to!

It was interesting. Some people were like, "I've never heard of you." A few people were like, "Oh my gosh, Erika, I love 'Stars.' That song was amazing."

I thought, *Are you kidding me right now? You really know who I am?*

The next day, we had to take a short flight out of Bahrain and then drive to the USS *Enterprise.* It was in port and we were going to walk onto the ship. It was a ninety-minute drive through the desert, where there was nothing but sand and

120-degree-plus heat. It was so hot that the air-conditioning in the car couldn't keep up.

Suddenly, out of the vast sea of sand, a United Arab Emirates checkpoint appeared like a mirage. We were surrounded by men in military fatigues carrying automatic weapons. We all got out of the car and went into a carpeted room. And I don't just mean carpeting on the floor. There was carpeting on the walls and ceiling, too. If something went wrong in here, would anyone hear us scream?

They checked the cars and our documents and let us through. There weren't any problems, but just being with a group of women and gay guys in a conservative country was enough to make me very nervous. I didn't want any unnecessary attention.

We finally arrived at the *Enterprise*, which they call "The Big E." Seeing it up close is like those movies in which people come to New York City for the first time. They just look up at the skyline, simultaneously delighted by and petrified of the enormity of the whole thing. Once we got inside we were taken to "Flag Country." It's a part of the ship reserved for the admiral, the highest ranking officers, and their guests. We were in shorts and T-shirts, and everyone else was in full military regalia. I felt embarrassingly underdressed.

They were happy to have us onboard. They showed the

dancers and the glam squad to their bunks, which were just tiny beds crammed into a little room. And this is an old aircraft carrier, so there was no air-conditioning on most of her. (You call an aircraft carrier "her," because she's powerful and not to be fucked with.)

Meanwhile, Admiral Carter, the highest ranking officer onboard, showed me to my quarters. I don't know where the admiral slept, but it couldn't have been any better—I got a queen bed, air-conditioning, and a TV. This was the lap of luxury. There was even a huge Marine posted outside my door, to make sure I was safe.

The only caveat was that this room was high up on the ship. "Listen, when you sleep in here at night, don't be afraid if you hear some crazy stuff," he told me. "The flight deck is right on top of you. So don't be worried." Yeah, that was a good warning to get in advance.

We had a female public affairs officer (or PAO) assigned to us. She gave us a tour of the whole ship, and we had the time of our lives. I got to pick up the red phone, which allegedly was a direct line to the president (though only to take a selfie). Our guide told us that the *Enterprise* was the first nuclear-powered aircraft carrier. (This was 2012, and the ship would eventually be decommissioned in 2017 after fifty-five years of service.)

We watched as they put fighter jets onto these giant elevators and raised them onto the flight deck. We ate a lot of Pop-Tarts, which apparently are very popular at sea. This is because they keep forever in their packaging and, well, they're delicious.

Our assigned liaison introduced us to several of the crew members onboard. They told us about their jobs and how they ended up in the military. We heard from men who left their small towns because there were no jobs, and the only way out was the service. I talked to a young father who was doing this to support his wife and two kids back in the States. We were all inspired and moved by the sacrifice of these men and women keeping us safe in the Persian Gulf. They live a tough life so we can sit our fat asses on sofas, drive SUVs, and take our freedoms for granted.

The next day was the Fourth of July. We were going to be performing on Steel Beach, which is the flight deck. They transformed it into a place for R & R. Imagine what a day off must be like for these people, since they can't leave the ship. By this point, we were out of port and cruising. People were playing music, throwing footballs around, just trying to have a good time.

There was a small stage set up for us, and we trotted up

there. We were wearing jean shorts, crop tops, and boots in bright colors. We keep it real classy for the Fourth of July. There was a clutch of people standing around watching. They weren't dying to see Erika Jayne specifically. They were probably just wondering, who were these broads walking around the ship in short-shorts for the past few days?

The problem with the performance was that the ship was moving. On top of that, we were against the wind, which kept blowing my hair back into my face. Just imagine trying to dance and sing on a moving ship while trying not to fall over in heels *and* having a mouthful of weave. Because the ship was moving, I couldn't really focus on the audience or else I'd get vertigo. So I was trying to look out to the horizon, but then I would get lost in the vast expanse of sea in every direction.

John, my sound guy, tried to record the show, but the temperature was literally 127 degrees. The camera didn't quite melt, but it did fog up and stop working.

Our performance wasn't the best of my career. We soldiered on (pun intended) through the whole thing, and the audience was polite, if not blown away. We did the job that we were there to do. If laughing at us trying to sing our stupid songs on Steel Beach while looking a mess brought even a little bit of joy into their lives, then mission accomplished.

You know when you hear service members say, "I was really pushed in training and now I know I can do anything." That's how I feel about this performance. I can wear a full weave and a full costume in 127-degree heat, dance my ass around in heels on a tiny stage at sea, against the wind, while trying just to concentrate on one focal point so I don't fall over. Bitch, bring me any stage on this Earth and it can't be as bad as that.

Yes, our show was a challenge, but the rest of the day was great fun. We spent it with the sailors while they had their barbecue. We helped them to a little slice of home halfway around the world. I've never felt more American on any Fourth of July as I watched our flag whipping in the hot, blue sky, blown by the same wind that had earlier in the day wreaked havoc on my hair.

While we were relaxing with the sailors, the admiral came by to thank us and tell us that the next morning we'd be leaving by carrier onboard delivery, or COD, plane. These are the small planes that deliver personnel, supplies, and mail from the mainland to the carriers. Because the runway is so short on an aircraft carrier, all the planes take off using catapults that help fling them into the air. Remember *Top Gun*? It's really just like that.

The admiral told me we'd be taking off at about four Gs.

"Put your feet on the seat in front of you and tuck your abs like you're doing a crunch, and you'll be fine," he advised.

That last night on the carrier, everything was winding down. The sun finally set, giving us a bit of relief from the heat. My dancers, my whole crew, and I went up to the vulture's nest. It's the round, bucketlike structure that is the highest point of the ship and is used as a lookout.

You could feel the stillness in this huge expanse of ocean. We looked out, and there was nothing to see in any direction except water and the rippling reflection of the full moon. It was so calm and peaceful. Which was ironic, considering there were six thousand sailors below us keeping this floating fortress in operation. Everyone was quiet and we just tried to take it all in, to savor the experience together.

I thought about our earlier show. I thought about all of our bad shows. All the times I'd fallen down, or the lights went out, or I had to deal with some shitty promoter who didn't have his act together, or some cop who had an ax to grind because he thought I was too sassy. But those are the things that make my job worth it, too. They make me stronger and better. Those are the things that fuel me to keep putting myself out there time after time.

Without all of those mishaps, I wouldn't be able to enjoy it when it's going well. When I have that glow deep inside my chest, when the audience is having as much fun as I'm having and pushing up against the stage like hungry dogs. Those victories make all the defeats seem insignificant. That's why I'll never stop. Every time, I have something to prove. Not just to the audience, but to myself.

13

BEST PIVOT OF MY LIFE

*J*ust before I was cast on *The Real Housewives of Beverly Hills*, I had secretly quit Erika Jayne altogether. The idea had been swirling in my mind for some time. I thought it was time to hang up my catsuits and settle back into the quiet life of being the wife of a successful attorney.

I started Erika Jayne in 2007. I had been performing everywhere I could, releasing songs, and gaining traction for eight years. Finally, after making the "Crazy" and "Painkillr" videos with Mikey, I felt like I had exhausted my personal network. I had talked to every producer, manager, songwriter, and choreographer that I possibly could. My inspiration was waning.

Through a friend of Tom's who is a music industry veteran, I scheduled a meeting with one of the biggest music managers ever. I figured I'd meet with him and see what he said before making the final decision about quitting. It was summertime, and I was wearing a supercute black jumper when I pranced into his office. I thought this was going to be a talk about numbers. I knew to keep the project going I would need to make some more music, do a few more videos, and book some more show dates. I was planning on running the numbers by him to see if they made sense.

When I sat down in his office, he had a massive whiteboard behind his desk with a roster of all of his clients and what they were working on. These are the biggest superstars in the world. Not only was I impressed with the names, I was impressed with the giant whiteboard itself. I made a mental note to buy one.

As we started talking, I laid out my whole case. I debated about how to further my career, and he looked at me across the desk and said, "Yeah, that's cool. You can do that. I know who you are and what you do, but I don't really think that this is where you should be."

He explained that I could get back on the treadmill and do what I had been doing all over again, but I probably wouldn't get more spectacular results. It's like I had reached the ceiling with what I could do by creating and releasing my own music.

He was confirming to me what I was already thinking: I was running out of possibilities for advancement.

Then he said, "I just feel like when you're in a situation like this, you should pivot."

Pivot? I didn't quite understand. For a second, I thought he was telling me that I should take a 180-degree turn and run away with my tail tucked between my legs.

I got into the car and had my driver take me home. In the backseat I thought, *You know what? I'm done with this. We've done a ton of shows, we've made a ton of tracks, and we've traveled all over the world. I made money and I did a lot more than anyone thought I would ever do. Maybe there's nowhere left to go.*

I had a long, hard conversation with myself. Maybe that manager was right. Maybe all good things must come to an end. He wasn't telling me to stop being creative or stop being myself. But he had convinced me not to drop a ton of coin on making a whole new album that might not do any better than the last one.

Erika Jayne had become less of an inspiration and more of a drag. The return on investment wasn't really making sense anymore. I came to it with no expectations other than to express myself, make some records, and get back onstage. I did all of that. I gained a cult following and sold a bunch of records. But the bullshit disappointments were becoming a little too common. The whole process was beginning to feel a bit rote. For a few days, I was feeling very sorry for myself. I was trying to figure out what to do once I sent Erika Jayne to that big, bubblegum-pink boudoir in the sky.

Maybe I'd finally go to college. That's sort of the running joke I tell about my career path. Since I never went, whenever something goes wrong, I always say flippantly, "Well, I could always go to college." I'm the only member of my family without a college degree, so I never got the collegiate experience the rest of them did. I have this vision of myself walking across the quad of some campus in a hoodie, sweatpants, and a backpack. My hair would be in a ponytail and my only makeup would be some blush and lip gloss. I'd be friends with everyone, and they'd all love me. It's like my own fantasy version of *Legally Blonde*.

But I don't think I'll ever really go to college. What would I even do after that? Like I'm going to take a bunch of classes and suddenly become an accountant? Please.

About a week after that meeting with the music manager, Tom and I were driving to Malibu. We were going to spend an afternoon with David Foster and his then-wife, Yolanda.

Our good friend Robert Shapiro, who became famous for his involvement in the OJ Simpson trial, had introduced us to David years before and we had all become friends.

In the car on the way to their house, there was something strange in the air. We were driving along the Pacific Coast Highway and all of a sudden, this extreme calm came over me. I was wearing a vintage Journey concert T-shirt, my Rick Owens leather jacket, a pair of jeans, and Christian Louboutin pumps. Tom was next to me in a pair of navy blue slacks and a baby blue shirt (which makes his blue eyes sparkle). Usually I'm pretty animated and can't sit still, but this day I was serene and staring out at the ocean.

When we arrived, Yolanda was sick as a dog, battling Lyme disease. She had on her famous cream bathrobe that fans of *The Real Housewives of Beverly Hills* saw her wearing all the time that season when she was quite ill. We sat on her sofa, opened a bottle of wine (obviously Yolanda wasn't drinking), and were just having a nice, leisurely chat.

Finally, Yolanda asked me how my music was going. I told her my frustration about where it was headed and the meeting I'd recently had.

And then the strangest thing happened. It's as if I could see something come over Yolanda, like a force taking over her body. She had no makeup on and her hair was tucked behind her ears. She was looking as simple as she possibly could. As I was rambling on, I could see the gears turning in her brain.

"Have you ever thought about being on *Real Housewives?*" she asked me when I finished.

"No."

She was holding her cell phone and started typing out a message right there. "I'm going to text my boss and let him know that he should talk to you about being on the show."

Looking back on it, that is what that manager meant by pivot. *This* was the pivot. He was telling me basically what I've been telling myself ever since I started my pop career: *There's another way to do this.* That manager challenged me to find yet another way. It wasn't until after I'd gotten the job that I realized *this* was the way.

Yolanda told me she wanted me to have a conversation with Alex Baskin. He's one of the partners at Evolution Media, which produces the show for Bravo.

Tom was sitting across from me and finally said, "What's *Housewives?*" I swear to God—one of the most brilliant legal minds in the country, but he has no idea about pop culture. (Even now he's more likely to watch *The Real Housewives of New York City* than me and my crew.)

"It's this reality show we're on," David told Tom. I can't make too much fun of my husband, because I had never watched the show, either. I knew what it was and I knew that Yolanda was on it, but I had never seen an episode.

I told Yolanda to give Alex my number and that he should give me a call if he wanted. Then I sort of forgot about it.

A few days later, Alex called me. We had a ten-minute conversation during which he explained the show and the casting process. It was almost like a legal discussion, as if he was saying, "Full disclosure, this is what the show is about. If you want to discuss it further, let me know." At the end, he asked me if I'd come in and tape something, so they could see how I look on camera. I said sure.

I've been on tape a million times for a million different auditions, and I know that sometimes it leads to a job. More often, it leads to nothing. After our call, I still wasn't seriously considering that this would happen. I was in a very neutral state about the whole enterprise.

The next day, I called Mikey, because I call Mikey every day. He mentioned my visit with David and Yolanda. "Did you guys talk about music?" he asked.

"No, not really," I said. "We talked about *Housewives.*" I paused for a minute, and there was an electric silence coming from Mikey's side of the call. I said, "I think I'm going to go and meet with the producers on camera."

"What? The fuck are you talking about?" he exclaimed. He was curious and excited at the same time, because Mikey has watched every episode of every *Housewives* franchise ever.

"Yeah," I said.

"Just from this conversation at the house?"

"Yes. That's it. I talked to her boss about it yesterday."

"You're fucking kidding me, right?" He knew the power of reality TV. He'd even been on a few different reality shows himself. But he never thought I would be interested in doing it.

"I don't know what's going to happen," I said. "But we're pivoting, right? We're pivoting."

I went into the Evolution office, and I was waiting for my appointment. I pulled out my phone and started to watch the beginning of Madonna's Virgin tour. I had seen it live in 1983 in Atlanta and watching it always makes me feel good. In that moment, I wanted to feel good. I sat there watching Madonna sing "Dress You Up" with the sound off.

Then I went in for my taping. I was just matter-of-fact, open, and very honest. I was unbothered by the whole process and was simply being myself. They asked me a lot of questions and were prying into what my life was about. It felt like an on-camera deposition, with lots of questions about life and how I see relationships.

They had already started filming the season with the other women. I knew that I was under consideration for the job and that they'd be moving fast. They gave me a window in which I would hear back.

It was a very hot summer afternoon. I was with Mikey and my assistant, Laia. They were both really excited about the possibility, but they're my biggest cheerleaders in the whole world. I could say we're doing a fucking fair in Pomona, and they'd be excited about it. Anyway, they wanted to be with me when I got the call.

We were running errands all day in Beverly Hills. As we walked around together, eventually I said, "Guys, I don't think they're going to call today. Let's go home and meet up tomorrow."

On the way home, I pulled into the 76 gas station on the corner of Crescent Drive and Little Santa Monica Boulevard. It's full service, and I hate to get out of the car. I was sitting in my Aston Martin while the attendant filled the tank. The phone rang.

"Hi, Erika, this is Stephanie Boyriven at Evolution," said the sweet voice on the other end. "I've got some good news. We want to offer you the full contract."

"Oh, that's great. Wow," I said. "Thank you so much." At the time, I had no idea what the "full contract" was. That I would be "holding a diamond," as they say, as a full-fledged member of the cast.

I called Mikey right away. "Oh my God, what's happening?" he blurted out.

"They offered me the full contract," I said.

He didn't say anything to me. Instead, he told Laia, who was still with him. They just started screaming into the phone. I hoped that he wasn't driving, because he and Laia sounded like they were jumping up and down.

Mikey and Laia are the two people in my life who were the most excited for me when I got the job. Tom and my son both have plenty of their own stuff going on. They were happy for me, because it was a great opportunity, but it's not like either of them were obsessed with Bravo. When I called Renee to tell her about it, she said, "Oh, that's cool. I've never watched the show before, but I guess I will now." You guess? Thanks for setting your DVR for your only child, Renee!

It only took about two weeks from when that manager told me to pivot for me to sign a contract to be on *The Real Housewives of Beverly Hills*. Here's how it happened. A couple of days after Stephanie called, I was on location filming my first scene. I showed up that day, and there was a contract there for me to sign. I called Tom. "Babe, there's a contract here," I told him.

"Great. Sign it and turn it in," he said.

"Do you want to read it?"

"No. It doesn't matter. They're doing more for you than you're doing for them at this point. Just sign the paper and hand it back."

I did, and the producers on set were a little confused. They said no one had ever done that before. A few days later, they made me sign the contract again. They wanted to be absolutely positive that I had checked it out before giving it back to them. I didn't read it the second time, either. In fact, to this day I don't think I've ever read it. I might have signed my soul away and had no clue at all. Oh well, who needs a soul anyway?

My first day of filming was with Yolanda and Kyle Richards, one of the original stars of the show. We were going for a walk in the park. I will always have a soft spot in my heart for Kyle, because she was so kind to me on that first day. She has been on the show forever. She could have been a real bitch if she wanted to, but she was very nice and welcomed me. I'm very thankful.

Before filming started, Yolanda gave me some really good

advice for my new life as a Real Housewife. "Be yourself," she told me. "Be authentic. Don't ever let anyone push you into something that you don't feel comfortable doing or saying."

She also told me to watch my words. "Be clear, focus, and remember what was said around you and what you say, because you will be held accountable for that later," she said.

That first season, I was a little blind going in. I didn't watch the show, and I really didn't know anybody except Yolanda. I think that was a blessing and maybe the key to my success. I was able to sit back, observe, get to know people, and see how they operate.

That's something I learned from being a performer for so many years. I knew I just had to wait, and my moment would come. When you come in and try to push, you get into trouble.

Someone asked me recently, "What advice would you give to a first-time Housewife?"

I said, "Shut your fucking mouth and listen." There's so much backstory, there are so many subtleties. There's the show and then there's your relationship with each woman beyond the show.

When I first started filming, I watched, listened, and learned. Then I just took it all in for what it was, which is this incredibly complex experience.

People who haven't been on the show don't really under-stand all of the time that the cast spends together. It's not just the footage that makes it to the final program, it's all the other moments that go unaired. On top of the footage on the cut-ting room floor, there's the cast photos, our travel time during trips, and chilling in the car with each other on our way to events. And we still see each other around town and at parties during the "off-season," or we text and email with each other to keep in touch because we are—believe it or not—actually friends.

The other advice I would give is that person had better be ready to be embarrassed. When you sign your name on that paper, you'd better be prepared to look like a fool, to be made an idiot, and not to be shown in your best light. It's an inevi-tability. You can't cry when that happens. You have to learn to take it or else get out of the game.

Everyone is going to have those moments like I had in Hong Kong, when I screamed at Eileen Davidson. There comes a point in every Housewife's life when the frustration takes over. Each personality expresses itself in a different way: some yell, some cry, some get mad, some get quiet. It's best not to close up, because for the sake of the show, every woman needs to open up and express herself.

I express my frustration through tears. I don't ever want

to lose control and annihilate someone. Those tears in Hong Kong were me trying to find the balance between saying how I really felt and expressing my anger. I felt I wasn't being heard, and that what I was trying to say had morphed into something else. That's why I exploded on Eileen when she said something so innocent.

Staying levelheaded and calm is my MO, but I can be very sensitive. I try to take things as lightly as possible, but sometimes you've just had enough. Each season it's harder to brush things off. You get to know these women, so when it gets turned around, it can become a mindfuck if you allow it. What they see as fair game because it's "just a show" can feel like a real betrayal.

I think that each Housewife is very unique in the way she reacts to the pressure of the show. Some are going to be themselves and take their own advice and be authentic. Others are going to listen to the supposed leader of the pack or those who have been there the longest.

Those you think are leaders actually might be followers. You want them to take a stand against what we all know is less than good behavior, but sometimes they're committing crimes of opportunity. When someone needs to be defended or told to stop, some women think, *But does this benefit me in some way?*

It's very calculated self-preservation, rather than just doing the right thing.

It's a very Machiavellian way of looking at things. Some in the cast are always tending their position in the hierarchy. Some of the women are one way when you're having an unguarded personal moment, and very different when the camera comes on. For someone like me, that is difficult. I don't want to embrace that person. I feel like I could never trust her.

There are some fun times and close bonding moments. Then, in the heat of an argument, when you think someone will advocate for you, they don't. I don't expect anything from anyone at all. When people stick up for me, I'm shocked. It doesn't feel like they necessarily would all the time.

Some people will keep your secrets and look out for you. Some wouldn't piss on you if you were on fire. And I'm not just talking about my cast. That's a recurring theme among the Housewives of every city. Yes, the players are different, but *every* cast goes through the same shit.

However, at the end of the day, if it doesn't come out of your mouth, you don't have to answer for it. If it does, you do. I think every Real Housewife needs to take responsibility for her actions and how she treats others, no matter what happened or how she feels she was provoked.

Filming can be lots of fun, though. There are moments when we look at each other like, "Are you fucking kidding me?" There are moments when we die laughing at each other, because we appear so stupid. Sometimes we look bewildered and confused by whatever foolish behavior is happening in front of us. That's the best. When you look at the other girl and you laugh, thinking, *You're going to cringe at that in about six months.*

Those are the times when you want to say to someone on the cast, "No, no, no, no. It doesn't have to be like that. You don't have to do that. You don't have to say that. Calm down." Those are also the worst times: fighting with people you care about, seeing people hurt, going through things that you know suck. And then know that they're going to have to relive it on television.

That first season, Lisa Rinna told me, "It's one thing to film the show. It's another thing to watch the show."

Now all of a sudden, I'm going to watch myself on playback. I'm going to think, *Wait a minute. Hold on. That's not what I meant.* Sometimes the shit that made perfect sense in your brain at the time does not translate on television. You knew you were right in that scene, but then you just come off all wrong. You know people are going to have a reaction to that.

I'm a huge fan of professional wrestling. I love to joke that wrestling is exactly like *Real Housewives*. They're both soap operas with treachery, betrayal, love, romance, hatred, flamboyant costumes, and of course lots of fights. Both in wrestling and on *Real Housewives* there are people that the audience roots for and people that the audience loves to hate. Both are wildly entertaining, and in both cases, the injuries are real.

Even though it's entertainment, it hurts because it's our lives. I think most of the audience thinks that they know us 100 percent. Because we're on television, they feel like they understand us completely. But they've only seen a small part of our lives. They can't imagine that we could be any way other than the way we're presented on TV.

That said, we have absolutely great fans. It's amazing to me how many people are fans of the show—many of whom you would never think would be watching. Because she'd seen me on *Real Housewives*, Christina Aguilera asked me to sing at her birthday party. That's insane. It really speaks to the reach of the show.

In February, I was in New York, seated at a restaurant doing an interview. The waiter brought a note and told me it was from a couple in the corner. It read, "Hi Erika. I didn't want to bother you, but I want you to know that all the New York academics are in love with you."

I looked around and saw these two brainiacs. They looked like they could be professors at Columbia. They waved politely, and I waved back. I was so flattered that after my interview, I went by to introduce myself—and of course take selfies.

I'm fortunate that from the start of my experience with *Real Housewives*, I've gotten a very warm reaction from the fans (well, at least most of them). I think that if people give me a chance and get past the blond hair, big boobs, stage makeup, and whatever insane look I'm wearing that day, they see a very relatable, normal woman. I come from a middle-class family in Atlanta, and only have a high school education. I have an over-the-top quality to my personality, but at my core, I am a very regular person. Albeit one with two airplanes, which I think people also enjoy.

As much of a hassle as it can be to make the show and let my life be so public, I'm getting something out of it, too. When we're in the middle of a season and I'm swirling in a sea of drama, the thing that gets me out of bed and in front of the camera again is the endgame. As I've said a zillion times, with *Housewives* I was able to take Erika Jayne out of the clubs and put her in America's living rooms. My project has exploded since then, with bigger bookings, business opportunities, and monumental exposure. Hell, you wouldn't even be holding this book without *Real Housewives*.

There are a lot of things to be gained by subjecting yourself to appearing on reality TV. There's some exploitation in the trade-off, but it is mutual. Even though what we trade is personal—the stories of our lives—it's ultimately a business relationship.

And you know what? It's the smartest pivot I ever made.

14

TOO MUCH WOMAN

At Center Staging in Burbank, I was rehearsing a new number with my creative director, Mikey, and my tireless assistant, Laia (who is a professional dancer herself). We were in the middle of preparations for 2017's Fort Lauderdale Pride performance when I got a call from my then-manager, Katie Mason Stern.

"If they had an open spot on *Dancing with the Stars*, would you want to do it?" she asked.

"Yes!" I said immediately, without even thinking about it.

"Well, it's all very last minute, and it's going to happen very fast," Katie said. "I'll get back to you."

I hung up the phone and said to Mikey and Laia, "Guys, I have a chance to be on *Dancing with the Stars*!"

They didn't say anything and looked at the floor.

"Guys, this is a great opportunity," I told them. "It will be so much fun and I'll get to dance and learn ballroom. I've never danced with a partner, but I've been doing this all my life. I can figure it out."

"I don't know, E," Mikey finally said. "I'm not sure it's going to be what you think it is."

"Come on," I said. "It's national television. Think about how many people are going to get to meet Erika Jayne for the first time."

"Okay, fine," Mikey said. "I'll support you no matter what. But I'm not sure you'll like it."

I wasn't going to turn it down. I just wasn't. I didn't think that an opportunity like that would come again. I'm one of these people who always says yes because I believe that everything leads to something great. But Mikey was right. *Dancing with the Stars* turned me into someone even my closest friends wouldn't recognize. Hell, I didn't even recognize myself.

I got the call from Katie at about three in the afternoon, and by six I was cast on the show. She wasn't kidding, they were not messing around. The next morning, the news came out that I was a part of the show's twenty-fourth season.

While filming the reunion special for *The Real Housewives of Beverly Hills*, I got a chance to talk to my fellow Real Housewives Lisa Rinna and Lisa Vanderpump, who had both already participated on the show.

Lisa Rinna was very excited for me. "It was the best time of my life," she said. "And I was in the best shape of my life. You're going to have so much fun and you're going to do great."

Lisa Vanderpump had nothing but good things to say about the show as well. "It's the hardest thing I ever did in my life," she admitted. Now, everyone sees Lisa Vanderpump as the grande dame of Beverly Hills. Let me tell you something: she is not some frail motherfucker. If she said it was the hardest thing she ever did, I knew I was in for some serious labor.

Hard work never bothered me, though, especially when it is in preparation for a performance. My partner on *Dancing*, Gleb Savchenko, is just like me. He's competitive, works hard, and puts everything out there for the audience. He also has one of the most beautiful faces I've ever seen in my life. You can tell from TV that he's attractive, but when you get up in there, it is something totally amazing. He looks like a movie star from Hollywood's golden age, like MGM royalty.

I have always been an admirer of the male form. Even so, I used to laugh when people would say, "Oh, Gleb is so sexy. Don't you get turned on being so close to him?" Hell no! We are there to be professional and to win. Neither he nor I are in any other frame of mind.

The first time we met, we were just getting a sense of each other. Within five minutes of him kicking my ass in that rehearsal studio, I had forgotten all about those matinee idol good looks. He was curious about what I knew about dance and ballroom and how well I could move. We were putting together a plan not just for the first dance, but for how we could work together for the season.

Soon it was time to start choreographing our first number. We were going to do a salsa to my song "XXPEN$IVE," which was released not too long before the show. Being able to dance to one's own song on a hit show was a really cool experience. It was going to be a great introduction to the world.

Gleb told me about an idea he had while at home watching his daughter Olivia play in their living room. She had this one toy that she absolutely loved and couldn't get enough of: a plush mechanical unicorn that walked. *Aha!* he thought. *Erika's like a unicorn. I want to open the number with her seated on a unicorn.*

Of course, I loved that idea. Just like Erika Jayne, a unicorn is a beautiful fantasy—and you're never going to see anything else like it. The whole routine was very much on-brand for me. I had a red costume dripping in glitz and diamonds and above-the-knee boots. Gleb wore a complementary red outfit, with the customary unbuttoned shirt. Compared to what my male backup dancers at Fort Lauderdale Pride would be wearing, it was absolutely chaste.

I need to give major props to the wardrobe department on *Dancing with the Stars*. They are absolutely amazing. Howard Sussman and his assistants, Daniella and Effat, were a joy to work with. They turn out dozens of killer looks each week with a moment's notice. It's mind-boggling how good and detailed every garment they deliver really is. They even went out of their way getting special lace for some of my outfits. If they didn't already have an amazing gig, I would hire them to make all of Erika Jayne's costumes.

I have a lot of respect for the hair and makeup team, too, even though Clyde and Preston, who do my hair and makeup, set my look for each performance. On show day we would all have to sit crammed in one half of a trailer all day, so no one would know what we were getting up to. This space was probably no bigger than six by ten feet, so it was tight. We shared a wall with Charo. We could hear her sitting alone in the other half of the trailer playing the guitar and rambling on in Spanish. (Luckily Laia is from the same part of Spain Charo's from, so she could translate.)

Sometimes the show's makeup crew would say something

like, "Erika, we're thinking about giving you a red lip tonight." I would relay that message to my team and show up with a red lip. "Was this what you were thinking?" I'd ask innocently. If you can say one thing about my team, it's that we're always two steps ahead.

The night of the first performance, I was nervous, but I wasn't freaking out. I walked in really assured. I thought, *I know what this is, I've got it. I'm going to get off this unicorn and do the salsa. I'm going to give it all I got. I'm dancing to my own song. How cool is that?*

It also helped that I knew there would be some familiar faces in the audience. My castmates Eileen Davidson and Lisa Rinna came to support my big debut. Lisa even brought her whole family. I was so excited for them all to see everything Gleb and I had been working on.

When I was backstage, I asked my fellow contestant and former Chicago Cubs catcher David Ross, "What's more nerve-racking, going out right now or catching the last game of the World Series?"

"I'd rather be at the World Series any day," he told me. "I'm scared to death, Erika."

My dance went off, I thought, without a hitch. I hopped off that unicorn, salsa-ed all over the place, threw my big blond curls around, and dropped into a split. I was feeling good.

Then we got to the judges' critiques. As I stood there pant-
ing and listening to their criticism, Len Goodman said he
thought the dance was "raunchy." I heard that word and it was
like a trapdoor opened underneath my stomach. It was everything I could do to remain standing. I wasn't mad. It was like
a giant pit of dread opened up inside of me. Not that anyone
would see it through my big smile and fake lashes.

You have to remember, this was coming off "Pantygate" on
The Real Housewives of Beverly Hills. We spent an entire season
talking about whether or not I intentionally flashed my vagina
at Dorit Kemsley's husband, PK, one night, while wearing a
black-and-white Mugler dress without any panties underneath.
(I did not, though Dorit and PK had a hard time believing it at
the time. Thankfully, that's since been resolved.)

I thought, *Oh God, not this again.* Given the tone, tenor,
and theme of his remarks, I felt like I was reliving the past season all over again in a single instant on live television. Dance
has always been an escape for me. Now I couldn't escape. It was
like everything I loved and that people love about me—being
sassy, bold, out there, myself—was now being criticized again.
From that moment, I knew exactly where this was going.

Still, we got twenty-four points. This score put us in the
middle of the pack. Not exactly what I was expecting when I
walked in so self-assured. As they cut to commercial, Gleb and

I had a chance to talk. He said, "Blow that off, don't listen to that. Don't let it get in your head. Fuck what he said. Don't give into that."

The pros on the show are psychiatrists just as much as they're dance instructors. They've all been through this many times before. They know the mental toughness it takes to get to the end of the competition. I didn't realize it then, but Gleb was trying to save me from myself and preserve our chances.

He was too late. It had already gotten into my head. I felt like I was being scolded for something I didn't do. What about all the other dancers? What about all the guys who took off their shirts? I barely touched my partner, and I'm being called "raunchy." Why was I being singled out?

I delivered what I always offer. It was a number that was fun, sassy, bratty, and sexy. That's showmanship. That's Erika Jayne, who they hired. And then, when she showed up, they told her they didn't want her. If you're penalized for being yourself, where do you go from there? I had no idea what to do next. I was unmoored.

I got home that night, and my son was sitting on the couch. Of course, he had watched the show to see how I did.

"They called you raunchy, huh?" he asked as I walked into the living room.

"Yeah," I said, somewhat defeated and still trying to process everything that happened.

"Fuck that guy," he said. "Mom, you have to remember, what are they going to say to you? Look at you. You have it all. They have to knock you down to size. They can't praise a woman who already has everything."

"I'm just mad they called me raunchy when everyone else was doing the same thing," I said.

"You're right," he said.

"I think it's because I'm too much woman and they can't handle it," I said.

"People don't like it when they think someone has it all," he said.

He was absolutely right, and this is something he learned through his own experience. His rookie year on the LAPD, he was told he did not belong because he came from wealth and had no idea what the life of a police officer is all about. Everyone he works with knows that his stepfather is a powerful lawyer and his mother is on television. But being in law enforcement is the only thing he's ever wanted to do his entire life, and he has an indomitable work ethic. He works hard and deserves to be there, no matter how big the house he comes home to at night may be.

The next week, we were doing the foxtrot. When we finally performed the number, my matte-black Lamborghini was brought out onstage. Gleb and I staged a scenario in which a hot cop pulls over a pretty woman. At the end, the judges called it a "Beverly Hills foxtrot."

I was hoping that my narrative on the show would be about a woman in her mid-forties still performing and having the best years in front of her. I thought people would find that inspirational. Now it seemed like I could never shed my title as Real Housewife of Beverly Hills. They were more interested in the perceived persona of a Beverly Hills Housewife than they were in me as a person.

That's when I realized that it was my persona that was being judged, not my ability. Val Chmerkovskiy, a veteran pro on the show, said it best: "The show isn't about dancing, it's about people." After that night, I didn't think I'd win no matter what I did.

Week after week, I could just feel the noose tightening. I told Tom not to come to the ballroom to see me dance. I had a bad vibe about what was happening and I didn't want him to see me like that.

What's worse, my shoulder started to hurt all the time. Going into the show, I was worried about my right knee. I'd had two surgeries on it to repair some dancing injuries—once as a teenager and once in my early thirties. I was convinced that if I got injured, it would be that. We were icing the knee every day after rehearsals. But that wasn't the problem. It was all the explosive upper-body movements of partnering that shredded my shoulder.

Gleb was starting to get frustrated with me, too. He knew I was talented, but he was impatient with me and disappointed at times. I would see him shake his head or mutter under his breath. I could see him tense up. He was begging me to get out of my own way. Even though he is sweet and encouraging, he'd had enough of me being in my head. At some point, it came down to a professional Russian dancer dealing with a middle-aged brat. Let's be honest: that would be tiring.

The next week, we got through our jive without incident, and I hate the jive. With all that soft shoeing and hand waving, it's very tricky and always looks very Vaudeville to me, even when the best dancers in the world are doing it.

Again, our score put us somewhere lost in the middle. Then I started to get paranoid. I allowed the looks I received in the ballroom—from the other contestants and from the huddling producers—to get to me. I allowed my imagination to run wild, inventing all the novel ways they were probably making fun of my cha-cha.

I also committed the cardinal sin of looking at some of the comments on social media. "Who the fuck does this bitch think she is?" someone wrote. "You guys thought she could dance well? She can't," someone else said. "She thinks she's better than us," another person chimed in. I know the first rule of the internet is never to read the comments, but it seemed like a lot of people wanted me to fail. They enjoyed seeing it. They enjoyed watching me be slowly, agonizingly consumed.

The next week, Gleb and I had a confrontation in my car on the way to rehearsal. "I really need you to break out," he said. "I really need you to show everybody what you're made of. I really need you to show up."

Immediately, I started to cry. I didn't cry because I was sad, tired, and hurt (though I was all of those things). I cry when I get angry. I cry because I can't put my fist through a wall.

"I can't connect," I kept saying to him. "I can't connect." I was so unsure of myself that I couldn't find my place in the competition. I couldn't get close to the audience. A great performer will make anything feel incredibly intimate, whether it's in a small cabaret or a giant arena. It's something I've been able to do on occasion, when I'm feeling my material and really in my element. Here, I totally lost that ability and felt adrift.

That week during rehearsals, Gleb had reached the end of his rope with me. The theme was "My Most Memorable Year," so we picked 1989. That was the year I moved to New York to follow my dreams of becoming a performer. We were going to do a cha-cha to Madonna's "Express Yourself."

He thought that if I were able to dance to a song I loved, by an artist I really admire, it would reinvigorate me. Even though Madonna is one of the holy trinity to me—along with Michael Jackson and Prince—I was still struggling in the rehearsal room.

Some of the other contestants were much more raw and revealing in their interviews. They talked about suffering miscarriages, surviving cancer, or helping with sick parents. I think the producers always have their favorites to win, and they really like that bravery and willingness to be vulnerable.

I could have done that, too. I could have talked about my father denying me to my face, my divorce, or my grandmother's death. Hell, I could have done a whole dance about Pantygate. But I didn't want to capitalize on any of those stories, at least not there.

I chose a different route. I wanted to uplift people. I wanted to show them that you can still dance in your midforties. You can still be fun. The best days are ahead of you, not behind you.

After a long week of tears and pain in the rehearsal room, our dance was well received. We got a thirty, our highest score yet. Still, the judges were telling us they wanted less "sex-pot." How are you going to take the sexpot out of a Madonna song? That's like taking the meat out of a hamburger. Finally, I told them right there on stage, "I am what I am. I'm not going to tone it down."

I felt a small amount of triumph saying that, but then Gleb and I were the last ones to be called safe that night. The noose was getting tighter.

I thought this was the beginning of the end for Gleb and me. He refused to believe it. The next day at rehearsal, he said, "Being called last doesn't mean anything. I've been in the bottom before and gotten out of it." He told me not to count myself out just yet.

Still, at next week's performance, I showed up with a bag packed. If we were eliminated, we would have to go on the promotional tour the next day. Gleb saw my bag and said, "Put that bag away. You won't need it. Having it is bad luck."

"I'm not going on *Good Morning America* looking like a fool," I told him. I wasn't going to be caught dead wearing a bad outfit. I even booked tickets to New York for Mikey and Laia, just in case I needed them to travel with me.

Our final performance was for Disney week, where each contestant dances to a song from a Disney movie, often dressed in character. We were doing a waltz to the song "Unforgettable" from the movie *Finding Dory*. I was hoping to get Cruella de Vil or at least Rapunzel from *Tangled*. I wanted to be a villainess or a princess. I could identify with anything but Dory, the fish who can't find her way home. As soon as we got that assignment, I knew the die was cast. They were going to help me find my way home.

Underneath my sea-blue gown, I was taped up so my shoulder would stay in place. I was in considerable pain, especially since for most of the dance I kept my arms perched upright in hold. We swirled around the dance floor like we were caught in an undersea current. I have to give props to wardrobe again, because they made me the most gorgeous costume to go home in. I knew who was rooting for me, and it was the costume department.

We got the best reviews of our time there. There were no comments about me being inappropriate or that my dancing was too Beverly Hills. "We really saw you open up," the judges told me. "Forget princess, you were a queen." We also got thirty-two points, our highest total yet—and once again, in the middle of the pack.

At the end of the episode, we were sent home. When they announced that we were cut, I turned to Gleb and said, "See, I told you."

As soon as I got backstage, I started crying. Once again,

it was that angry cry. I had let the whole experience get away from me and get *to* me. I was sad that my essence, which is over-the-top, fun, and sassy, was made to seem snobby, mean, and divisive. Also, honestly, I was sad that I lost. Who likes losing?

Heading back to my trailer, I ran into Gleb. He was with his wife, Elena, as well as his daughter Olivia and her friend. Olivia was dressed as Belle, her favorite Disney princess. It just broke my heart.

"I'm so sorry," I told Gleb, trying to keep the makeup from streaming down my face. "This is the night your daughter came, and I made her see her father get kicked off the show."

"What are you talking about?" he said, very matter-of-factly in his Russian accent. "That's life. She needs to know the way the world really is."

While we were clearing out our crammed trailer for the last time, the show's travel coordinators came by. They told me which overnight flight to New York I'd be on. As soon as they did, Laia said, "Erika, Mikey and I are *coincidentally* on the same flight!" Like I said, my team is sly. And this way, I'd have some company on the very long journey.

On the flight, I barely slept. I felt frustrated and angry. It didn't help that whenever I tried to sleep, my shoulder was constantly spasming.

The next day, we did our interview on *GMA*. They gave me a little disco ball trophy with a unicorn on the top of it. I named the unicorn America. That way, I figured if America wasn't going to give me their votes, at least I could finally say, "I've won America!" I paraded that thing around JFK and LAX, showing it off to the world. I really do love it.

When I got home and talked to Tom, he was supportive. But you have to remember that he's a very stoic and pragmatic guy. When I voiced my concerns about how I felt I had been portrayed and how I felt like it was unfair, he said, "You're looking at it all wrong. You need to be looking at it from this perspective, which is millions more people know who you are now. Whether getting sent home was right or wrong, it is beyond your control. It's not your show."

What really concerned Tom was how I was dealing with my injury. I thought my shoulder really hurt when I was dancing, but once I stopped using it, the pain got even worse. I was taking all sorts of pharmaceuticals and it wasn't even touching the pain. Tom is not a nervous Nellie, so when he said to me, "I need to know what's wrong with your shoulder," I knew it was time to get it checked out.

I went to a new orthopedist. When I saw that he looked exactly like Doogie Howser, MD, I knew he was going to be good. He believed my shoulder had been under stress from all of those years of dancing, and this period of intense use just exacerbated something that was already happening. He came up with a plan to put Humpty Dumpty back together again.

The biggest lesson I learned from the whole experience is that there is such a thing as being too much woman. There is. Most of America doesn't want real, raw, brazen sexuality in their faces, especially from a woman my age. You're seen as cheap or slutty or "raunchy." What they want is cute: cute smiles, dainty figures. Erika Jayne is a lot of things, but no one will ever call her "cute."

The people involved with the show were absolutely wonderful from start to finish. I became friends with everyone else on the cast, from David Ross, whom I still direct message on Twitter every now and again, to my neighbor Charo, the legend who paved the way for other "cuchi-cuchi girls" like me. Everyone was in the same boat, and we were all kind and supportive to each other. I think the love that's in that room is the one thing people need to understand.

The professional dancers were great, too, but they're doing a job. Once we've all left the ballroom, they're going to have another cast of beginners to whip into shape and psychologically figure out. All of the pros work their asses off, and that always earns my respect.

Maybe I took losing too personally. But I take everything

personally, even when they tell you not to. It's just who I am and how I look at the world. I didn't expect to win, but I didn't expect to walk out questioning everything I ever built.

I'm so glad that it happened, though, because it restored my faith in Erika Jayne. The whole experience was like stripping a house down to its studs. I could just collapse it, or I could rebuild it and keep going. And when Erika Jayne was laid bare to the frame, I saw that she was made of steel. To knock her down for good, it was going to take something a lot stronger than this.

This season, I'm happy to root for Gleb and his new partner week to week. And if they ever wanted Erika Jayne for an all-stars season, I'd be there.

15

GOING TO THE CHAPEL

My family has always been Protestant, but my father and my stepfather were both Catholic. It was important to my stepfather that I be raised Catholic.

I was baptized at seven and had my first communion shortly thereafter at Corpus Christi Catholic Church. I didn't really have any say in that, because I was a little kid. After that, I had years of religious education at CCD, the Confraternity of Catholic Doctrine. It's the Catholic church's equivalent of Sunday school. When I was enrolled in Catholic middle school at the Immaculate Heart of Mary, we had CCD as part of the school curriculum. Eventually, it came time to get confirmed with my entire class. But I wasn't feeling it.

I always felt like an outsider at that school. It was as if they were all normal and I was different. That school is where I had my first mean girls experience, with some of my classmates making fun of me and passing notes about how much they hated me. These were the same girls who were going to get up on the altar at confirmation and talk about being good Catholics. It smacked of hypocrisy to me. They wanted no part of me, and I thought they were all sheep. They passively went along with whatever the people wearing the robes were telling them to do.

I also thought it was bullshit that we were essentially forced to make a lifelong commitment to a religion when we didn't know any others. At thirteen years old, how could I possibly make all these big promises in front of God about being Catholic for the rest of my life? I knew enough to know that I didn't know anything. Just because the teachers at school and the priests were telling me this was right for me didn't mean that it was. What if I wanted to be a Buddhist? What if I wanted to be a Protestant like my grandparents? What if I wanted to become a Scientologist? I don't think I would ever want to, but it might have helped my entertainment career—who knows?

I felt like I was being punished for even questioning why we would get confirmed. If one of the priests could have given me a valid explanation as to why we were doing it, I would have been happy to participate. But we were expected to follow blindly. The fact that they said we should do it was supposed to be enough of an incentive. They wanted us to do what we were told. Well, not me.

One day after class, I told my religion teacher, Mrs. O'Connell, "I'm choosing not to be confirmed." She was surprised but kind of blew it off. When we got closer to the ceremony, she realized I was being serious. She told the principal about my decision. The principal called my mother down to the school for a meeting.

When Renee arrived, they told her that she had to force me to get confirmed. "No, I'm not going to do that," she told them. Renee and I had plenty of issues, but she always had my back when it came down to it. "Listen, I've done everything I possibly can. There is nothing else for me to do if this child is not going to do it, and that's that."

I was the only kid in my class not to get confirmed. I never quite understood why no one else had the hesitation I did. I looked around at my classmates and wondered if I was the only person who felt this way. Or maybe I was just the only kid who had enough guts to say, "I'm not going to be forced into this." I wanted my peers to challenge or at least question authority. And I was determined not to be a sucker.

I didn't care what any of them thought: my mother, the

priests, the principal, my friends. I knew I made the right decision for myself. I decided to attend the confirmation ceremony
to support my friends. When I got to the church, my friend
Amanda said, "Maybe we can ask the priests to give you a blessing, even though you're not getting confirmed." She asked the
priest, and he said no.

The Catholic church always made me feel judged. I saw
church as a place of limitations and harsh criticism. A place
where I felt like I would be corrected or ashamed, like I was
bad. I never felt the church was loving or inclusive.

My husband, Tom, was born in a Catholic hospital and
went to Catholic schools all the way through law school. He
still sits on the board of trustees at Loyola University Law
School. But he was taught by the Jesuits, an order of priests
that believes in education and teaching people to question the
things around them to find the truth. The priests molded this
man and encouraged him to help people whenever he could.
His experience with the Catholic church was worlds away from
mine.

When I enrolled in public high school, I left the church
behind. I didn't really miss it until I was twenty and about to
get married to my first husband, Tommy. We had a huge ceremony at St. Patrick's Cathedral in Midtown Manhattan where

Tommy, a New York native, had been baptized. In order to get married in the Catholic church, we both had to get confirmed, so we did it together. Tommy and I had a private confirmation ceremony in the chapel underneath the altar at St. Patrick's.

As part of the confirmation process, I had to choose two things: a confirmation name and a sponsor. A confirmation name is like a second middle name that one adopts, which is also the name of a saint. Mine is Ann, after my grandmother. I chose Christine Olender, my mother's best friend and one of the managers of Windows on the World at the World Trade Center, as my sponsor. We shared a lot of similarities in our lives and she was the best Catholic I knew. It was a special moment with her by my side. It became even more poignant to me after Christine lost her life while at work on September 11, 2001.

A few years later, I was getting a divorce. That is something that Catholics frown upon, and that judgment turned me off of organized religion. But I have spiritual beliefs that I cherish and stand behind. I believe in faith. I believe in God. I believe in angels, or at least a force of good in the world that we can feel.

I tend to believe that we live many lifetimes. I have no proof of this yet, obviously, but ask me again in my next life. I believe that the soul can never be destroyed, but it simply transfers. I believe in a higher power. I don't believe in hell as a place of eternal damnation with a lake of fire and the gnashing of teeth, but I do believe in hell on Earth. I believe that there are people who suffer needlessly and that we should try to alleviate that suffering.

I believe in the first lesson any kid learns in CCD: the Golden Rule. I treat people the way I want to be treated. I try to confront everyone with kindness and will be nice to them as long as they're nice to me. I don't fuck with anybody who doesn't have it coming to them.

Life should be about treating people well and trying to find the good in others. To evolve the humility it takes to look out for others. I don't know any other way to say it. Not looking out for others just shows a limited soul and low maturity level. No one knows what someone else has been through. We don't know their story. We don't know where they've been or where they're going. We don't know their potential or whether the path they're on might lead them somewhere great. That's why I try to treat everyone like an equal.

Trust me, I fall short of that mark every day. That's such a Catholic idea, though. No matter how hard we strive for goodness, we're all sinners on the inside. Just ask Erika Jayne. She's even a sinner on the outside!

I think it's important to pray. It's important to have some sort of spiritual practice for your own soul. I say my affirmations every morning when I wake up. Every night when I go to bed I say my prayers, what I'm thankful for, and I ask for protection and guidance.

I met with a spiritual adviser awhile ago. She said to me, "You don't pray for your mom."

"No, I don't," I said.

"You have to correct that," she said. "That's not right. You have to pray for your momma."

"Really?" I asked. "I pray for myself, my son, and my family. Isn't that enough?"

"No," she said. "You have to pray for your mother specifically."

I think she was right. I do believe that the words we say out loud and the prayers that we think manifest themselves in the real world. I'm not just talking about the scientific studies that prove that prayer helps heal sick people. I'm talking about how our intentions can influence reality.

When Tom and I were restoring our house in Pasadena, there was a strange area that was kind of like a bathroom with a little gym attached to it. We had no idea what to do with the space. By that time, I had been collecting icons and religious art for a while. I thought it would be great to put all of them in a little chapel.

I brought up the idea with our interior designer and she

loved it. Now it's my own meditation room, my spiritual space. I think that it's important to have a place like that where you can go and quiet the mind and think about things. That's what that space represents to me. It's my private spiritual sanctuary.

I use it as often as I can, but not enough. Rather than going to the chapel, I usually say my daily prayers in bed right before I pass out from exhaustion.

When I do sit in there, I close my eyes. I try to slow down my mind. I let the darkness behind my eyelids wash over my consciousness. I let my mind expand, atom by atom, out across the chapel and through each room of the house. It goes out past the gardens of our estate, past the freeways of Southern California, past the ocean in the west and the mountains in the east. It glides over the land and through the sky, taking in the whole world.

It travels to everyone who is important in my life. My husband, who has given me so much and taught me so much more. My son, who I am so glad grew into a strong, good man, but whom I will always want to protect. My mother, the cause of so much of my strife but also the source of so much of my character. My grandmother, who taught me how to be a leader and always to follow my heart. Mikey, who inspires me every day to be a fiercer version of myself. Travis, who believed in me and changed my life forever.

Then my mind travels backward in time, from my sometimes chaotic childhood to the stability and joy I found performing in children's theater. From the hard times of auditioning in New York to the success of birthing Erika Jayne into the world. From not knowing how I was going to make ends meet in LA to having the love and security of Tom, the best man I've ever known.

Then my mind travels to the future, which is as unknowable as the blankness behind my eyes. But it's bright, too. There are stars of possibility illuminating that darkness. All I have to do is pluck those stars, one at a time, from the sky. I can hold each of them in my hand and make that vision come true. I see that ball of light resting in my palm and expanding, blossoming into something great.

We never know what is going to come. When I was a child commandeering the lead role in the kindergarten production of *Mrs. Jingle B*, I never would have imagined that I'd be a wife and mother living in California. Reality shows didn't even exist yet, so there was no way to conjure up starring in one. The wealth, happiness, friendship, and love that I've found on my journey was nothing but a mirage back then, but they're real now. I've kept my dreams alive and achieved so many of them. It wasn't by compromising. It was by constantly battling back the fear that I would be criticized and judged for being true to myself and my vision.

As I sit in my chapel with my eyes closed, I wish for the future and dream of it. A million pictures flash through my mind in fleeting moments that may or may not actually occur. I'm open to all of the possibilities—good and bad. I let the beauty of that uncertainty wash over me like starlight. It's so wonderful and intense. I would have no idea how to contain it if everything that happened until now hadn't prepared me perfectly.

ACKNOWLEDGMENTS

First of all, I need to thank my family. Renee, I'm at this great place because of you. You always believed in me and told me that I could do anything, and I will forever be grateful for that.

Mr. Girardi, you are truly magic and I hope that even a little bit of that magic has rubbed off on me. You are the best teacher I have ever had in my life and I would never have the balls to do what I do without your constant love and support.

To my son, the unconditional love that we share for each other is the greatest blessing in my life.

Without a great team around me, my whole life would be impossible and this book would have been, too.

Thanks to Travis Payne for reminding me of what I love, encouraging me to get back in the game, and not letting me wither on the sidelines. And Peter Rafelson for making music with me and helping me create a sound.

Mikey, you are there every day and keep taking Erika Jayne

to a higher and higher level. We will forever be bonded. From the tiniest of dumps to the biggest stage on Earth, you always make me feel like I am a star. You always treated this project like it was some Madonna-level shit, even when we were just starting out.

To the most fabulous Armenian in my life, my publicist, Jack Ketsoyan. I love you and thank you for believing in me all these years.

Laia is the glue that sticks everything together. I couldn't do anything without you. You're the Erika Jayne to the real Erika Jayne.

To everyone who has started me on the Real Housewives journey, starting with Yolanda Hadid. It all goes back to that unexpected day on your couch in Malibu. Thank you for opening up Erika Jayne to the world.

Andy Cohen, thank you for appreciating me for exactly who I am. No one gets it like you do. Thanks to Doug Ross, Alex Baskin, and everyone at Evolution Media for embracing me and bringing me into your crazy reality family.

A shout-out to everyone at CAA, especially Santini Reali and Mark Mullett, who brought me into the fold. This book never would have happened without Cait Hoyt. Hey guys, more deals please. We've got lots of money to make.

Thank you Gallery Books, Simon and Schuster, and our

very patient editor, Jeremie Ruby-Strauss. (Even though you had no idea what a circuit party was before reading this book.) Also, thank you to Jen Bergstrom, John Vairo, Lisa Litwack, Jen Long, Brita Lundberg, and Jen Robinson.

Thank you, Brian Moylan, for listening to all my bullshit and turning it into something I hope people will enjoy. You are so insightful, clever, and capable of conveying subtleties anyone else would miss. That's why I wanted you to write this book with me. I needed someone like you to get past the facade and find the humanity behind all of these crazy stories. We popped our book cherry together!

All of this would be for nothing without my fans. Thanks especially to all of those OG supporters who loved Erika Jayne before the Real Housewives. To all the new fans and followers, thank you for allowing me to entertain you. It is my sincere hope to inspire you and make you smile. I appreciate your constant support and it never goes unnoticed.